The Outsider

The Outsider

A Personal Journey

BRIAN MAYFIELD-SMITH
WITH IAN HEADS

Pan Macmillan Australia

First published 2000 in Macmillan by Pan Macmillan Australia Pty Limited
St Martins Tower, 31 Market Street, Sydney

National Library of Australia
Cataloguing-in-Publication Data

Mayfield-Smith, Brian, 1947– .
The outsider.

ISBN 0 7329 1061 7.

1. Mayfield-Smith, Brian, 1947– . 2. Racehorse trainers – Australia – Biography. 3. Wildlife conservationists – Biography. 4. Wildlife conservationists – Africa – Biography. 5. Environmentalists – Africa – Biography.
I. Heads, Ian. II. Title.

798.40092

10 9 8 7 6 5 4 3 2 1

Typeset in 12.5/15 pt Bembo by Post Pre-press Group
Printed in Australia by McPherson's Printing Group

Internal design by Gayna Murphy, Greendot Design

To my wife Maree, who encouraged me for years to tell this story and who has been a huge influence on my life. To all the animals who have been wantonly killed and cruelly treated by humankind. Why, as a species, have we been unable to evolve beyond this?

CONTENTS

INTRODUCTION xiii

CHAPTER ONE
The Place Where God Showed Off 1

CHAPTER TWO
Kids' Stuff 11

CHAPTER THREE
The Rebel 21

CHAPTER FOUR
Wild Days Up North 33

CHAPTER FIVE
Animal Encounters 53

CHAPTER SIX
Travelling Man 60

CHAPTER SEVEN
Setting the Bar High 73

CHAPTER EIGHT
Heading South 81

CHAPTER NINE
The 'Big Smoke' 87

CHAPTER TEN
'They Tried to Steal My Horse' 92

CHAPTER ELEVEN
The Hand of Fate 98

CHAPTER TWELVE
The Day I Beat T.J. Smith 110

CHAPTER THIRTEEN
Some Horses I Have Known 116

CHAPTER FOURTEEN
I Did It My Way 130

CHAPTER FIFTEEN
The Thrill of Africa 139

CHAPTER SIXTEEN
The Place That Lives in My Heart 151

CHAPTER SEVENTEEN
Breaking Free 163

CHAPTER EIGHTEEN
African Adventure 175

CHAPTER NINETEEN
Into the Wet 203

CHAPTER TWENTY
Out of Africa 229

We patronise them for their incompleteness, for their tragic fate of having taken a form so far below ourselves. Therein we err, and greatly err. For the animal shall not be measured by Man. In the world older and more complete than ours, they moved finished and complete, gifted with extensions of the senses we have lost or never attained, living by voices we shall never hear. They are not brethren, they are not underlings, they are other nations caught with ourselves in the web of life and time . . .

Henry Beston, *The Outermost House*

Brian's Credo

I am not important as an individual, but what I do is very important. In a million years, the animals of the world—and the environments they inhabit—have never been under a greater threat than they are today. As humankind overpopulates, we force the animals to depopulate. The greed, indifference and injustice associated with this daily scenario spells the doom of these animals if all of it continues unchecked.

I have always thought of this book as a window of opportunity to highlight this outrage. I have heard many times the countering argument in the words: 'Do you consider animals as important as humans?' My answer is this: if you can't be productively compassionate to the plight of animals, any compassion shown to humans is a lie. Look into the eyes of any creature that is threatened . . . and you will understand.

I will not receive a single cent of monetary gain from sales of this book. It will go to endangered animals.

This is a book for the animals . . . it is not for me.

Brian Mayfield-Smith, August 2000

INTRODUCTION

Brian Mayfield-Smith's view of his own life does not match the views of those who know him, and know his story. Mayfield-Smith, one of the great horsemen of Australian racing's last thirty years, judges himself severely. Not for him is there resting on the laurels of past successes. Instead, there is an ongoing, restless search for meaning, a search that will surely last as long as he lives, to achieve something of real value.

The dual strands of his life make Mayfield-Smith one of the most intriguing figures in Australian sport. On the one hand, and it is remarkable enough, is the story of the taciturn racehorse trainer who came to Sydney from north Queensland with his trademark hat and bush lore—and performed a feat that still nearly defies belief. From 1985 to 1986, Mayfield-Smith performed the 'impossible' in Australian racing, ending the reign of the legendary Tommy 'T.J.' Smith as Sydney's number one trainer. Hard and ruthless, Smith had stood on that pedestal for thirty-three successive years. Mayfield-Smith went on to win the title twice more to prove he was no 'one-year wonder'. Mayfield-Smith's pleasure at beating Smith, a man who he says tried to do the wrong thing by him when he first came to Sydney, shines through in this book.

Only a few years before, Brian had been a one-horse trainer, broke and living in a tiny caravan under a spreading Moreton Bay fig tree on Cairns racecourse. There one afternoon, Mayfield-Smith declared his intentions to a pal: that one day he would move to Sydney and beat the great T.J. Smith.

The pursuit of this lofty goal, gathering momentum as he ploughed relentlessly south via stays at Townsville and Brisbane, the hand of fate always hovering somewhere close, is a truly thrilling story in its own right. And it is told in full in the pages that follow.

But ask Brian Mayfield-Smith, and he will tell you bluntly, as is his way, that it is not even *half* the story. Rightly proud of his achievements in racing, he was motivated by a far greater passion when writing this book. In 1995, Brian and his wife Maree shocked the Australian racing world when they announced they were closing operations in Sydney—and moving permanently to Africa to become involved in wildlife conservation. They had first travelled there on a holiday in 1987, and had had a shared epiphany about Africa's magnificent animals and the need to fight to preserve them. In Africa Brian found depth and meaning rarely present in his previous life. He went back again and again, finally making 1995's clean break as the racing community watched, open-mouthed.

This book tells of the Mayfield-Smiths' great trek—some 42,000 kilometres through eight African countries, and of the increasingly frustrating search for the 'right' opportunity, the disappointment tempered always by the beauty they found around them. Bowed but not beaten, Brian and Maree came home eventually, and slightly reluctantly, to a life in racing in Melbourne, figuring that by doing so they would at least be able to generate ongoing funds for their beloved cause, the animals. Brian chose to tell his story in the hope that the book's sales could further help this cause, and perhaps also assist with awakening realisation of the world's need to look after its natural resources.

Brian suspects the African 'thing' was in him from days way back, as a youngster in North Queensland. He recalls clearly the deep thrill that registered when he first saw the John Wayne movie *Hatari* in the Tropical Theatre in Cairns in 1963. (In Melbourne these days, the Mayfield-Smith four-wheel drive carries the number plate 'Hatari'.) Going back further still, he remembers a moment when a huge circus elephant gently plucked a Mintie from his hand at Gordonvale.

The Mayfield-Smith story is a tough and colourful one of a self-described 'outsider', a man more comfortable with animals than with his fellow humans, who has struggled restlessly to find meaning in his life. But he was absolutely determined that his story not be presented as any sort of sanitised 'heroic' yarn. For if Brian Mayfield-Smith has shown heroic qualities (and I would argue he has) his is a flawed heroism. His upbringing was difficult, due mainly to the treatment he received at the hands of a father who had been deeply affected by his World War II experiences. With little sense of his worth as an individual, Brian strayed to the outside edges of society. After leaving school, he headed for the backblocks—working as a stockman on remote cattle stations in Queensland's far north, and in the Northern Territory. At times they were drunken, brawling days, although there is no doubt that the rare 'connection' he has with horses was honed in those hard years. They were raw times, full of experiences incredibly distant from the lives that most Australians lead.

Mayfield-Smith's return to society—and eventually high

society when in racing he linked up with the likes of multi-millionaire man-of-the-world Robert Sangster—his great successes, and then progression towards the sense of calmness and real purpose he found in Africa, add up to a truly remarkable Australian story. What follows, then, is not a book about a racehorse trainer, although there are racing yarns in it, and the smell of the turf is around. It is about an extraordinary Australian who, against all odds, managed an extraordinary feat—and then, at forty-six, began a search for deeper meaning.

For Brian Mayfield-Smith, that search continues.

Ian Heads, August 2000

Chapter One

The Place Where God Showed Off

Years ago I read what someone (I have long since forgotten who) had once said—that Africa was the place where God showed off before he began creation. And that is how it seems to me. It is such a place; there is nowhere else like it in the world. You can feel it pulsing—the people, the cultures, the animals, the landscapes. The spirit is uplifting.

***

We reached our home away from home late on a balmy afternoon in January 1996. Mt Kenya towered majestically above, its jagged peaks snow-covered, the mountain rising massively and alone from the plain. Maree, my wife, and I were at a low ebb that day. For five months we had roamed around southern and east Africa in our four-wheel drive Land Rover, searching for the breakthrough that would be our new beginning and our future. Leaving behind a near-lifetime in the racing game in Australia, we had travelled to Africa with hope and enthusiasm in 1995, determined that we would tackle something of real meaning in our lives—planning to help African wildlife and, hopefully, the place and the people too. No doubt more than a few back home thought we were crazy when we dreamed out loud our vision of leaving Australia forever and setting up some sort of game reserve or safari camp in Africa. I had, after all, managed to make a serious mark in Australian racing, coming to Sydney from the Queensland backblocks to knock Tommy (T.J.) Smith off the perch after his thirty-three years as leading trainer. But we went anyway . . .

The trip we took, beginning in Nairobi, had been one of magnificent moments burned indelibly into memory, but it was also one of deep frustrations. Too often, it seemed, we were strangers in a strange land, battling mule-stubborn bureaucracy and impenetrable red tape to try to get anywhere close to what we had hoped to do. We had travelled far and wide, 42,000 kilometres across the land, through eight different countries, contending with the dramas of the 'wet' as huge storms rumbled around us day after day. It was my tenth trip to Africa, Maree's ninth. We had investigated half-chances galore, but found none that seemed right.

We hadn't said it in so many words to each other yet, but we knew we were beaten. This time, anyway. To surrender to the hopelessness we found, with the environment treated too often with disdain by governments wracked by endemic corruption, was a bitter pill to swallow. Basically we had reached the conclusion that the Africans didn't want us . . . they wanted our money. We were close to making the choice that we could not be part of that system. So, it was in a rather sombre, thoughtful mood that we drove through the gates of Jamie Roberts' property at Nanyuki, over which looms mighty

Mt Kenya with its peaks permanently snowy despite the fact that the equator runs virtually straight through the mountain. It is my favourite mountain. I know why the Kikuyu believe that *Ngai* (God) dwelt there. Maybe they are right.

Jamie was a great pal to us on that trip, a career pilot with an energetic approach to life who opened the doors of his house to us with great generosity. A bloke with plenty of Australian 'bushie' in him. 'If I'm not here, just throw your kit in—the staff will look after you,' he'd told us.

As it turned out, on this particular afternoon in January Jamie was at home, but readying for a trip. 'Great to see you guys,' he said. 'Look, I'm flying to the [Masai] Mara to my brother's camp to pick up some tourists to take them to Rusinga Island on Lake Victoria. Why don't you pack a small bag and come with me?'

We didn't need any further encouragement, and within an hour or so we were in Jamie's Cessna, 12,000 feet above the Aberdare Range, flying across the Rift Valley with its extinct volcanoes, with Lake Nakuru and Lake Naivasha away in the distance to our right, ringed with the pink glow of millions of gathered flamingos. Beyond the Rift, Jamie sent the plane into a steep descent, sweeping low across the wheat fields at an altitude of a couple of hundred metres, the ground below us a blur through the plane's windows.

On the way Jamie buzzed the farmhouse of a mate, sending the plane zooming across the property at just above rooftop level. 'That oughta get him out of bed,' he said, roaring with laughter. Jamie likes a bit of fun. Almost immediately, we were in a gorge on the edge of the Mau escarpment, beyond which the country drops down to the Masai Mara, wide, rolling country teeming with wildlife. Through the narrow gorge, which closed almost to wing-width at stages as we threaded the needle, we headed into open country, and a wonderful sight . . .

Through my window I spotted a mob of animals in some lightly wooded country. 'Elephants,' I shouted, pointing.

Jamie promptly threw the plane into a tight loop turn, pulling that many 'gs' it felt like your arse was going straight through the seat. Then we were behind and over them—a mob of about fifteen, the dust rising as they ran for the trees, ears back and their stubby little tails sticking out.

It was a fabulous sight . . . a moment to send the spirits soaring. In a single image it captured the unexpected excitement that is Africa—to people like Maree and me, anyway—the chance of seeing something wonderful around almost every bend in the road. The weight that was on our shoulders that day lifted in an instant. Our trip at that late stage had become something of an anticlimax. Our options had grown narrower with the passing days, and acceptance that we weren't going to find the answer in Africa—this time, at least—had begun to take over. Then, in the thrill of seeing these ancient, sensational animals, the disappointment was all gone in a flash. For both of us it became, let's worry about tomorrow . . . tomorrow. Let's just enjoy this. 'The trip is getting better all the time', I noted in the diary later.

The days leading up to our return to Mt Kenya had been especially tough. Weary from travelling, we had been caught out by the black-money dealers in Zambia and had been dudded. Although it was only a small, passing incident, I noted in our trip diary that we had gone 'swimming with human crocodiles'. Soon afterwards we had pulled into a fuel station in Lusaka and a member of the Zambian military had approached us and asked if we were interested in buying some animal skins. Very likely the bloke was a part-time poacher. Young men there had scoffed at our 'Tusk' conservation sticker on the Land Rover, driving home to us the reality of Africa—so many people there have no concern for the wildlife which means so much to Maree and me.

In Llongwe, Malawi, we had battled the immense frustration of trying to get access to funds in our bank account back home, an exercise continually thwarted by the clearance centre in Johannesburg in the late days of our trip. Our main source of income was a Visa card which the bank in Llongwe rejected. Without enough money to head back to a First World banking system in South Africa, we had to make a 'run' for Kenya, with a kitty of only US$300. Then, with funds dwindling fast, we encountered a fat, obnoxious pig of a border official as we crossed from Malawi into Tanzania en route to Jamie Roberts' place. He demanded a US$139 crossing fee from us—four months earlier, when we had first crossed that border, it had been US$65.

Car problems added to the nightmarish qualities of the late days. On the road one morning we blew a seal, causing the engine to spew coolant all over the windscreen. I bound it back together with a strip of inner tubing rubber which I kept for just such an emergency (a very handy accessory when travelling by car in Africa!). A hundred kilometres further on we encountered a brake drum problem which was finally 'solved' thanks to one of Maree's hairpins. Further down the road still, we came upon the scene of a road accident. A truck had ripped out one side of a bus. There was blood everywhere, and a body visible in the bus. A small accident, the police assured us . . .

We drove on through a storm as black as midnight, with great curtains of rain, to the town of Iringa. No sign of any accommodation was apparent as night fell, so we headed for the one light in town, the local service station. The proprietor kindly offered us a parking spot in the lubrication bay overnight, assuring us we would be safe there as he had security guards patrolling the place. At some time in the night, as we attempted to grab some sleep, a bloody great petrol tanker, complete with bogey trailer full of fuel, managed to jackknife right in front of the bay, effectively trapping us inside as the driver attempted to manoeuvre out. For more than twenty minutes the truck revved furiously, edging backwards then forwards as the driver tried to extricate the rig—all the time spewing out great clouds of diesel gas. Thankfully the exhaust pipe was on the far side of the truck from us—or he may well have put us to sleep permanently.

Surviving all this, we reached the Tanzania–Kenya border to find that our last US$50 was insufficient for the crossing permit. I headed back to the Tanzanian side with our final traveller's cheque, changing it to US$50 and some Tanzanian shillings. I then had to change this money into Kenyan shillings on the local black market. Finally, we made it back into Kenya. It was the easiest country in Africa for getting money on the card. Arriving that Saturday afternoon we had a strong feeling of being 'home' again.

Our time on the Masai Mara renewed and reinvigorated us. A fragment of the tour diary captured how it was at the camp run by Jamie Roberts' brother:

> We had a bit of a sleep-in and missed seeing a group of elephants which passed quite close to the camp, but we can hear them trumpeting in the nearby bush. It is a glorious morning with the birds calling as we look through the trees out onto the expanse of the Masai Mara. A group of zebra at the edge of the treeline look curiously at us, but are unconcerned by our presence. During the night we had heard lions calling, close by . . .

An exhilarating flight back to Nanyuki added to the magic of the experience in Kenya. Popping over the high wall of the Aberdares, in a buffeting headwind which had the plane pig-rooting, Jamie took us down to a couple of hundred feet as we skirted around hills and rocky outcrops.

Easing back down over the gentler descent on the other side—but still a bumpy sleigh ride, thanks to the wind—we spotted some rhino in the Solio Rhino Sanctuary, between the Aberdares and Nanyuki, and zoomed low over some *shambas* (small farms), with the people looking up at us as if to say: 'Who are these bloody *njingas*?' (a Swahili term that loosely translates as 'foolish people') before landing at Nanyuki airstrip in a rainshower.

Taking you to Nanyuki so early in this book but so far down the track of my personal journey (to this point) may seem like turning a life upside down. But it is the way I knew it had to start—in Africa, which had begun to creep its way under my skin probably more years ago than I can remember. When I was a skinny kid in North Queensland, the Saturday afternoon matinees at the Gordonvale Theatre would often kick off with a *Jungle Jim* serial, or something similar—the animals, the jungle, the baddies . . . pure rubbish, of course, but for us kids it was something special, another world, a world of great excitement.

When the movie *Hatari*, starring John Wayne, came out in 1963, I went to see it once in the Tropical Theatre in Cairns, and it captivated me so much that I went back and saw it three more times. Thoughts of Africa rested in my subconscious for evermore after that, I think.

But why Africa? people have asked. Because it's just so bloody exciting, that's why. And in my life I have always liked doing exciting things, even though I suppose that I have always regarded myself as being pretty ordinary, or extraordinary only in that in my life I have determined *NOT* to be ordinary. The quest for something exciting and different was what inspired me to take flying lessons at the Royal Aero Club in Bankstown. They cost me $18 an hour at a time when I was earning $30 a week as a strapper for trainer Jack Denham at Rosehill, but I liked flying. It scared me a bit, and I knew I was never going to be any gung-ho pilot. But I wanted to do it. So I lived on $12 a week, and went flying for an hour with the rest of what I earned . . .

Throughout my life I have always been a dreamer. It's probably why I was never a big star academically—I had trouble focusing on the smaller things. I have always liked to picture something grander. Call me an idealist, if you like. I always dreamed of being *somebody*, and the fact that I turned out to be a horse trainer of some note fulfilled that dream. But only to an extent. I always had the feeling—and I still do now—that I wanted to be someone who would stand out, someone who achieved genuinely worthwhile things.

Back now from Africa, carrying on life again in what has been judged a highly successful career as a horse trainer, the question nags at me: have I really done *anything* of significance? I'm nearly fifty-three as I write these words and I keep thinking, what am I going to do now? Have I missed the boat?

All that follows in this story pretty much comes down to one thing—a search to make a meaning out of life. I have always felt that I didn't want to be like a flower that blooms and dies, fills a space for a short time and then is gone. Life seems pretty bloody pointless if we just go whoosh, like that . . . like a train passing through a station. The things I have done—training racehorses and setting high goals, going to Africa to try to make a contribution—have been about trying to make sense and meaning out of my existence. In a way it's been selfish, and I thought of that in 1995–96 in Africa: deep down, am I really here to try to help these animals and these people, or am I just here for myself? A bit of both, I suppose. To an extent the striving is about being absolved—trying to put something back in, so you can have peace of mind and spirit.

Africa, and specifically its wonderful and endangered animals, is my motivation for writing this book. My hope is that telling of my experiences will perhaps send some others there, to see what I have seen. Mainly, I hoped the book may help, in smaller ways or larger, the fight that means so much to me—to help preserve the animals and the natural things of this planet. As far as I'm concerned, a world without animals would be no world worth living in.

Africa will always be part of the equation for me. I would hope that when the time comes for me to meld back into the earth again, it happens in Africa. That is important to me—that my remains finish up there, on Mt Kenya, when the inevitable end comes. Over there my life is more enriched, my spirit soars higher. There is no place on earth like it, and it draws me back again and again. The plight of its animals is the specific reason I decided to write this book. It is the main reason I continue to train racehorses in Australia. So, if this book is about an ordinary Australian life and the ups and downs of the ancient sport of horseracing, it is just as much about an extraordinary continent—and the animals that live there. And it is about how going there can change you forever, as it did me.

This, then, is my story. If people can identify with a knockabout bloke, a bloke who made at least something of life, made it interesting, achieved a little along the way, then that's fine. But the last thing I want to be seen as is some 'heroic' figure, with people asking, 'Jeeze, did this bloke have any faults at all?' As you will discover, he did . . . and does.

So, my story is presented warts and all, from the difficulties of my growing-up years under a father brutalised by his war experience and the medical treatment that followed, through school days, cattle station days when I was truly an 'outsider' in society, then on to the discovery of a certain gift for training and dealing with racehorses, and to the remarkable flashes of fate that carried me irresistibly from place to place, from opportunity to opportunity—and ultimately to triumphant years as Sydney's top trainer.

It is the story of a boy who loved animals, and loves them still, and who is more comfortable with them than with his fellow humans. And it is about Africa—the place that I knew I would one day come to—and the place that, finally, provided meaning in my life.

It will now begin, as stories should, at the beginning . . .

CHAPTER TWO

Kids' Stuff

My first memory is of a horse. Of several, actually—beautiful big draught horses, stamping and snorting and steaming in the carriageway of an old bakery somewhere long forgotten on the edge of Brisbane. I was perhaps three. My mum and dad were staying with friends in suburban Brisbane, people named Dilgers, en route to Innisfail, North Queensland. I recall there was a young girl, about six or so, and one morning the lady of the house said to her, 'Take Brian with you and go around to the bakery and get a loaf of bread.' The sights, the sounds and smells I experienced that morning have stayed with me throughout my life.

The bakery was one of those big old brick warehouses, with wide double doors. I can relive the moment now—being hit by the wonderful warm smell of fresh-baked bread as we walked through the big doors. And then, the horses. There were three or four of them, tacked up to the bread wagons with all the leather and fancy gear on. The wagons were brightly painted, with the baker's name stamped on the sides. They stood side by side, lined up along the big ramp where the bread was brought out from the ovens.

The effect on me was overpowering. Everything looked so huge, especially the horses. And it was a swirling, smoky sort of morning, maybe from the baking, with the haze adding an extra ingredient to the magic of the experience. To a young mind it all added up to a wondrous thing.

I have often wondered since whether my life's path, my destiny, was set in stone in that moment, on that day. Above everything else, it is the horses I remember most clearly—the look of them, the smell of them, the sound of them. I'm sure something was imprinted very deep in an impressionable mind. After all, there is no real history of horses or horsemen in our family, although my grandfather, Jack Williams, told me stories of his time in France in World War I when he was charged with the duty of looking after a horse belonging to one of the officers. There is no other link that I know of in my background, yet the fact of it is that I have been around horses just about all my life ever since. There is something that attracts me to horses. I just get a good feeling when I am around them. I have always felt that, mainly, they are the purpose for which I've lived my life.

⁂

I was born two years after the end of the war that changed the world forever. I greeted the world at Hobart Hospital on 24 May 1947 after a most difficult birth. As I learned many years later, the doctor attending said he had never seen so much blood, and he advised my parents, 'No more children after this one.'

The first-born to Norman and Mabel (nee Williams) Mayfield-Smith, I was in fact followed over the next dozen years by Lawrence (four and a half years later), Noel (ten years later) and my sister, Sharon (twelve years later).

The world was then slowly emerging from the shadow of the second great war of the century, but it was a shadow that lingered long enough to reach across my life. My father's war had been a bad one. An Air Force man, he was based at the dual American–Australian facility in Mareeba, North Queensland, flying bomber missions from there to take on the Japanese in New Guinea. On one such mission he was shot down, ending up alive but stranded in the depths of the New Guinea jungle.

It was an experience he never talked about much, but there is absolutely no doubt it scarred and shaped the rest of his life. Later, he shared fleeting fragments of it with us—through Mum, not directly with us kids—about how he and the other crewmen smoked banana leaf cigarettes in the jungle, and how they lived in deadly fear of the Japanese jumping out of trees and strangling them with piano wire. Somehow they escaped, being picked up by a boat on the shore of the Arafura Sea and being taken back to Darwin.

Shards of the war stories lived on in our family. My grandfather, Jack Williams, barely spoke of his experiences in France in World War I, but I never forgot one brief tale he told of Australian soldiers under heavy fire, lying flat on the ground in their heavy winter greatcoats. Some of the coats crimped up a little at the back, and afterwards they were found to be shredded with bullet trails, so low was the gunfire.

Many years later my mother would talk about how my father was when she went to visit him in hospital in Darwin. How she found him long haired, wild eyed and heavily bearded—and obviously desperately unsettled by what he had been through. Now and then he would leap up on the bed and yell, 'They're coming!'

My father, obviously, was never the same again after his wartime experience. His condition was bad enough for him to have to go now and then to Brisbane for ongoing treatment—electric shock treatment for his nervous condition. I can remember being with Mum when she put him on the train in Cairns.

Although my father and I were poles apart, I was always proud, even as a kid, of his participation and sacrifices in the war. I never told him so. I think now that I should have. I felt later that in order to 'do my bit' I should also contribute to this ideal of freedom that he had fought for. When my number didn't come up for National Service at the time of the Vietnam War, I went and volunteered for the regular army to try to get there. After a couple of hours of physical tests and interviews at the recruiting office in downtown Sydney, I was politely told that I wouldn't be mentally compatible with army life. In the aftermath of Vietnam, the futility of it, the waste of young men's lives—physically and mentally—brought about by the gross miscalculations of the situation by politicians who could so easily move onto the 'next issue', unscathed and remote from it all, I thought: How lucky was I? There but for the grace of God go I.

My father had a very, very short fuse—and the fact of my early life was that I got very severely disciplined a lot of the time. I think if any kid today had to suffer what I did, it would be deemed pretty solid child abuse. I got hit a lot—and hit hard. My father would get a big strap and belt the hell out of me; it wouldn't just be one or two hits, it would be a real flogging.

There are so many bad moments that stick in my mind. Once, as a little bloke, I'd shat my rompers, then tried to help my father clean the car—using the rompers. When he came around from the other side of the car and saw me, he went out of his tree, grabbed the rompers, and rubbed them into my face. Another time we were in the car, having a normal sort of conversation, I thought, and suddenly he sort of snapped and belted me full in the face, shouting that kids should be seen and not heard. And at dinner at home one night, with just my mother and me there, my father furiously smashed a bowl of spaghetti bolognaise on the floor, the food flying all over the room, yelling, 'Who wants it?!' These are just a few examples of how it was for me, growing up.

I don't blame my father for the way things were. I look on it now as a bad card that I happened to draw in my life. He had big problems to contend with, and there were no doubt others worse off than me. But I sure copped it. During the beatings my mother would be doing her best to get between us, trying to hold him off, yelling at him to stop. I suppose I regard him now with mixed feelings. I look back and ask myself the question: would I have been any better than he was if I'd been through what he went through? I honestly can't answer 'yes' to that.

As I said, there are people who have suffered a hell of a lot worse than me. But the treatment my father dished out in those early years no doubt shaped my later life to an extent. It was all very negative and it made me retreat into my shell. I always felt that people were looking at me, waiting for me to do something wrong. Increasingly, I found it hard to relate to other people . . . and I probably still do. The mental scars of earlier years are still there today. To be honest, I am still not comfortable in groups of people.

My father gave me no feelings of worth. In fact he hammered a sense of inferiority into me. He would constantly belittle me, crack down on me: 'You're trying to be perfect—you'll *never* be perfect,' he would scoff. My brain was programmed with the belief that I wasn't much good—and never would be. He would tell me I was 'antisocial' and 'had a chip on my shoulder'. Often he would be irrational: 'Get that,' he'd declare. 'You're not going out today. I'm keeping you in for the weekend and you can tell your cheesy mates to nick off.'

When you get that sort of message from an early age, it's hard to shake. I withdrew into myself, and when I went to school I found it difficult to make friends. I just felt that I wasn't worthy of being accepted by other people. I probably still feel a loner, an outsider, although the experience of the years has helped . . . you read, you learn, you can talk yourself into things. But there is still a problem there, and often my first line of defence has been to take an aggressive stance.

I copped it worse than the other Mayfield-Smith kids, although my father was pretty solid on Lawrence too. By the time Noel came along, things had eased off. I bore the brunt of it. My father was at his worst healthwise in the late 1940s and early 1950s, and I just happened to be the first kid. With the increased distance from the war years he gradually got better, and his realisation that my mother wasn't well probably played its part in that too. Still, he was a selfish man, although he worked to provide us with a good home and education. But kids need more than material things from their parents, of course.

Everything in the family seemed to revolve around him and when I was older I said to Mum more than once, 'You're not his servant—you don't have to do all that.' She would answer, 'He's my husband and I have to do what I have to do that's right for the family.' One thing that really used to piss me off was when Mum would pick him up from his workplace in town. There was a pub just down the road from our place, only three minutes from home. He'd get Mum to drive him there on his way home from work, and then we'd have to sit in the car for a couple of hours while he drank. When I was a bit older I'd get on the bloody horn and start blowing it. Eventually he would come out, and I'd be in trouble again.

My old man was a real garden freak. We had a great big back yard and he had garden beds dotted around everywhere. Often when I wanted to go out with my mates at weekends, he'd keep me in to work in the yard—to mow and rake and clip. One school morning he said to me, 'Listen, fella, when you get home from school, I want you to do those gerbera beds.' The beds were cut clean and neat, so I was a bit cheesed off and when I got hold of the shovel that afternoon, I just threw the dirt around. At the end everything was pretty much buried—you could just see a few leaves sticking out, and some flowers. When he got home, I was upstairs. He stood at the bottom of the stairs and screamed, 'Get down here, fella!.' I knew what was going to happen. Man, he gave it to me that day . . .

My father was from a fairly well-to-do middle-class family in Sydney and my mother was from North Queensland, part of the well-known sporting Nash clan. She spent her growing-up years in the sugar town of Gordonvale and in the old gold-mining town of Chilligoe. During the war my mother was in the Women's Army Nursing Service. The two of them met, like many other couples at the time, because of the war, when my father was based in Mareeba, up from Cairns.

For reasons I have never been sure of, after the war, they chose to make the long trek from North Queensland to Tasmania, via Brisbane. They were married at Murgon before heading on to Hobart, where they bought into a shop, staying there for two and a half years. I remember nothing of Tasmania. My early memories of the Brisbane bakery and, later, of a blue and grey dog in a suburban house there, came from the return journey 'home', a stop-off en route to a new beginning further north, when my mother and father (and me) were in transit from Tasmania to the next part of our lives, in North Queensland.

We ended up in the heart of sugar cane country, Innisfail—East Innisfail, actually—in a rented house sitting high on wooden stumps and surrounded by wide open spaces, real country. The house was a traditional 'Queenslander', with a creek down the back. It was a good place for kids. Not far beyond was the Johnson River where I saw a crocodile one morning, and a little ginger kitten mewing at the river's edge. I 'rescued' the kitten, convinced that the croc would surely have eaten it otherwise.

The McGregors lived in the house next to ours, local butchers who had kids and cows—and horses. There were no fences between the widely spaced houses, and I remember one of their cows getting under our house one day. Mum hunted it out with a direct hit on its bony bum via an accurately thrown scrubbing brush.

My mum was the strength of our family—a great person, really. Life was never easy for her. She'd had polio as a child, and in her early married life contracted rheumatic fever, weakening her heart. She was so bad for a time that I had to be sent away to school at Gordonvale, because she was too sick to look after me. I remember her collapsing one day near the bedroom door, and my father screaming at me to grab the tablets which were on a table next to the bed. Mum got cancer in her fifties, and she died at fifty-three. Coincidentally, my father also died at fifty-three, in April 1977, not long after I had moved to Sydney to tackle the big time as a trainer.

Mum did a mighty job with her family. She was the financial manager and even though we didn't have much in the way of money, her care enabled us to be a fairly comfortable middle-class family. Because of her frugality, we even managed to have a family car in the fairly early days in Innisfail. It was a little Morris Oxford with a canvas top. On the grille was its mascot, a badge representing a little red bull. Later we had a Vanguard, the model with the illuminated turn indicator that would shoot out from the side, and later still, in Cairns, a brand new Wolseley, testament to my mother's expertise in handling money.

She juggled things in her life so well despite her sicknesses: looking after my father (with his problems), helping out with other people (which she seemed to do all the time), and getting a good education for her children. If you talk about someone having grace in her life, then my mum certainly had it. She gave us our chance, and my appreciation of her has grown progressively through my own acquisition of knowledge and experience in life.

The horses next door to us in Innisfail were of greatest interest to me and the older kids would put me up in front or behind them, and take me for a ride. I was three. Four doors down from our house the street ended in a football oval. One afternoon down there I had got hold of a rope and was chasing a horse around. Suddenly the horse let fly and double-barrelled me, straight in the stomach, sending me flying backwards. It knocked the wind right out of me, but luckily did no other damage. I got up screaming blue murder, my cries fetching a neighbour at some speed from a nearby house and causing quite a stir.

Maybe that incident should have cured me of horses. It didn't. Somehow they were already imprinted on my brain, and even then, as a little fella, I would get excited whenever I saw one. The snippets of early memory I hold onto seem to be mostly about horses. Right now I can conjure up in my mind's eye two horses tied up under a lemon tree on a scorching hot day. One of them has only one eye.

A year or so after we had gone north, we packed the Morris and made the long trek south to Brisbane, via the inland route. I was still only a little fella, but I clearly remember three things from the trip. Somewhere along the way we stopped beside a creek to have lunch, and I found a turtle which we put in the boot of the car. Later, when we went to get the turtle out, he had climbed up into the panelling and we had a hell of a job trying to retrieve him, which we finally did. I remember, too, Mum telling me at one point that the next big town we were to drive through was Charters Towers. I immediately had visions of this magical place with great towers rising from the plain. Charters Towers is not like that, of course, and our arrival there did not live up to my expectations. My third memory is of a mob of cattle on the road completely surrounding our little car. What I remember most about that, though, is the fact that my old man was wearing a handkerchief, knotted at the four corners, on his head. I remember thinking how stupid he must have looked to the stockmen.

Years later, on another of our overland trips (we made at least three of them, that I remember), something interesting happened to me, something I have never forgotten. I was about ten years old at the time, and we were heading back from Brisbane, on the road near Rockhampton. It was late afternoon, with the sun setting behind a stand of dead trees, and suddenly this feeling of nervousness and unease came over me. Something changed in me at that moment. Never again did I view life as I had as a carefree child. When I think back on it, I feel it was at this moment that I changed from being a child with no cares to someone else, someone I didn't really understand, but who just wasn't a kid any more.

Chapter Three

The Rebel

My second early-childhood memory is of a dog, a blue and grey dog, maybe a spaniel. It belonged to people named Tracey, friends of my mum and dad in Brisbane. I don't remember the people at all, but I remember the dog. Probably that says something very telling about my life, the fact that I have always felt more comfortable around animals than I have around people.

My best friend in my early years was a dog, a border collie–kelpie cross named Boxer. At the time we were living in Stratford, Cairns, and on the day we went to pick out a pup, the one I wanted kept climbing under the timber boards of the house we went to. Eventually my old man said, 'C'mon, you'll have to take this one here,' so we left with another one of the litter. I think the reason I wanted the rebellious one was because he was harder to get.

But the one we took home was a lovely little dog and he became a source of great friendship and emotional support for me. If I struggled in my dealings with people at times—well, my mate Boxer was always there, undemanding, courageous and loving. I remember well the day he got his name. We'd had him a couple of weeks then and still hadn't given him one. But one weekend a friend of the family from Gordonvale came to stay—a knockabout sugar-cane cutter named 'Boxer' O'Grady. I remember we were all out the back one morning mucking around and Boxer O'Grady sort of grabbed me. The little dog ran straight in and nipped him on the thigh, breaking the skin. 'The bastard bit me!' said Boxer. From that day, the dog had his name. Boxer.

Everywhere I went, Boxer went. And he would always take my side. If I ever got into fights—which I did from time to time—he would always try to help me out. Boxer used to get into his own scraps too. He was black and tan, with a tail that curled and stood up high. If he was ever in the middle of a big mob of dogs you could always spot him by the tail. I remember him getting into a fight with an Alsatian down outside the pub one day, and finishing up with a big patch out of his neck and skin off everywhere. Another day, out the front of our place, a bloody pig dog got hold of him and we were flat out saving him.

As a young bloke I used to get the rail motor—a small commuter train—to school, along with all the other kids. Boxer would always accompany me up to the station, and in the early days he'd chase the train along the tracks, almost all the way to the next station, Aeroglen, a Cairns suburb out near the airport. One memory can still bring tears to my eyes: me as a kid, looking out the rear carriage of the train at the little black figure struggling along the tracks determinedly, way behind. Of an afternoon, he'd wait out the front of our house at the top of Mason Street in Stratford. When I came around the corner about half a mile away, he'd take off and tear down the street to meet me. I was five when we got him and he was my mate until my tenth year.

In the end, a tick got him, one of those little red scrub ticks that can poison and kill. They were a problem up there and we used to check him all the time, swab him with kerosene and so on. One afternoon I was in a canefield near our place with some horses, and Boxer came looking for me. He was lame and I took him home to Mum. 'I think he's got a tick,' she said, 'but you'll have to wait until your father comes home from work; then we can take him to the vet.' The delay probably made all the difference. Boxer lay in the dirt under the steps to the house, with his head down. I can see even now the little clouds of dust that he raised with each breath. We finally got him to the vet, old Mr Denny, and he told us, 'I can give him an injection, but he might be too far gone.' Boxer died there soon afterwards, on the table.

I was shattered. I had just lost my best friend.

* * *

School days started for me soon after we moved to Cairns, to a house at 21 Mason Street, Stratford, which backed onto hills and bush. Higher up in the hills was a waterfall which trickled lazily for most of the year, only to roar down as a sea of brown and white foam when the wet season came. I used to love that. The house at Stratford was home to me more than our place at Innisfail had been. There were lots of horses around, and as a youngster I desperately wanted to own one. 'You'll never own a horse, Brian,' my father would say. I don't really know what took my folks to Cairns. Maybe my father was just chasing a job. He worked for a time in the Northern Builders Supplies hardware store in Lake Street, and eventually went to the Cairns Regional Electricity Board, working in the office there.

I was four and a half when my parents put me into Grade 1 at Our Lady of Good Counsel school in North Cairns, run by the nuns. Starting school was a pretty traumatic experience, but like all kids I eventually got used to it. More or less.

At this, my first school, the discipline was extra tough—and the beatings that were by then a fact of my life at home continued. The nuns had canes cut from the tough and pliable Lawyer cane which grows in the bush up there. It would sting like hell when you got whacked with one, which I did often enough. I got plenty of 'doings' in my time at Our Lady of Good Counsel. I remember a day in front of the whole class when I was in big trouble. One of the nuns grabbed hold of me by the hand so I couldn't get away, and laid into me. I was yelling and dancing around and she must have belted me around the legs at least ten times. Oh, yeah—they were pretty solid, those nuns. If they decided to discipline you, they could really dish it out. I wondered later whether it was a bit of their own frustration with life coming out. I'm sure God didn't tell them to do it.

I even copped it when I was learning to play the piano! I was never real happy with that, anyway—it was my mother's idea. I felt a bit of a sissy, carrying this bloody music case around while my mates were up there in the bush, or knocking around with horses. Even for little kids then there was a very 'macho' attitude to life. If you got hurt, you didn't cry—you just grimaced. You couldn't look weak, whatever happened. And playing the piano didn't quite fit that image. I've got a certificate from the Trinity International College of Music in London, though, to prove that I got at least a little way along the track of becoming a musician.

But even doing that I copped a hammering. Mother Manignes from the school used to take the piano lessons and whenever I hit a wrong note, which was fairly often, she'd whack me hard between the shoulder blades. At other times she'd use a wooden pointer to follow the sheet music, and when I made a mistake I'd cop it right across the knuckles.

In the year my mum was really sick, I lived with my grandfather and grandmother, Jack and Charlotte Williams, in Templeton Street, Gordonvale, and went to the state school there. I was twelve years old. Until I was eleven I attended St Augustine Boys' School in Cairns. Eventually I went on to the Mt Carmel Christian Brothers College in Charters Towers. One thing was consistent at least—I got a hammering at all of them. I suppose I was a mischievous kid. Although I never went overboard in the things I did, it certainly was apparent I gave people plenty of reasons to belt me. When I look back on it I've got to think I was doing things wrongly enough, often enough, to upset those in charge. The beatings had the effect of hardening me up, even as a little kid. It hurts, but then it gets to a point where it doesn't hurt any more, if you know what I mean. Eventually the fear was taken out of it for me. I would say to myself: I've been through this before . . . I can handle it.

As a little kid I had been much impressed by the stories in a set of encyclopaedias my old man brought home one day. I particularly liked tales about the Spartans, and the one that especially stuck in my mind concerned a kid who knocked off a fox, or some other animal, and had it under his tunic. When he was confronted by a man demanding to know what he had under his shirt, he replied, 'I have nothing.' The adult could see the animal struggling under there, but didn't say anything. By the time the boy got home and opened his shirt, the animal had cut him to ribbons with its claws. Yet he had not cried out in pain, or complained. He had borne it stoically. That philosophy appealed to me greatly.

Even as a little bloke I was very determined. I would dig my toes in. Even my loving mum gave me a whack now and then. 'You determined little monkey,' she'd say out of sheer frustration. The thing that period of my life left me with, for sure, was a chip on the shoulder. I got into lots of fights, at school and beyond. I had a fiercely competitive streak and there was pride too. If someone took me on I always felt I had to respond, and in those days the solution to my problems was to do my best to 'sort someone out' rather than talk about it.

At St Augustine's, which I attended as a day pupil, a run-in with a lay teacher named Murphy one day early in my stay brought me a painful beating. At St Augustine's they forced the religion into you. Looking back, it was a real brainwashing exercise. I remember one of the teachers talking about God one day and I asked him, 'How do you know God is really there?'

'Because the scriptures tell us so,' came the answer.

'But they're only books . . . written by people,' I said. 'What proof do you have?'

He droned on about miracles and all the rest of it, but I still wasn't satisfied. So then he asked me a question:

'How do you know New York is there?' he asked.

'It's in the atlas,' I said.

'Well . . . that's a book!' he declared triumphantly.

'But we've been taught it here at school!' I said.

'Look . . . SIT DOWN!' he said, exasperated.

I tangled with the teacher Murphy when he got me up in front of the class and asked me a question relating to something written on the blackboard. 'I don't know the answer,' I said.

'Put out your hand then,' he said—and gave me six hard cuts with the cane. 'Now, stand over there and when you *do* know the answer, tell me.'

After a while he came back to me. 'Have you got that answer yet?' he asked.

'No,' I said. So he gave me another six.

It went on until I had had twenty-four whacks with the cane. That night one of my hands swelled up like a balloon. This was enough to bring my mother storming into the school the next morning, seeking out the head brother. 'If you ever let this happen again, I will have my solicitor straight out here,' she told him. The solicitor in question was a fellow named Bede Mellick, a big wheel in Cairns. They didn't touch me for three months after that, but in no way was it the end of it.

* * *

About the only time my old man ever took an interest in me was when I played sport. Cairns back then was a big town for soccer, many migrant families having moved into the district for the cane, both as growers and cane-cutters. I started in Saints 3 soccer side, then progressed pretty quickly to Saints 1. Most Saturday nights I'd get a mention on Cairns Radio 4CA for my goal-scoring exploits. My old man really got into the soccer—he'd be on the sidelines cheering and screaming.

I think the fact that his son was a pretty fair soccer player gave my father a feeling of pride, and of acceptance with his mates too. He worked at the brewery for a while, Cairns Brewery, and a few of the senior soccer players worked there as well. To have a son scoring some goals helped my father become accepted by the others there, I'm sure.

Later, my success as a horse trainer, which came quickly, provided some common ground between us. We were never really close, but he did become proud of me. I remember when, in my first year as a trainer, the race caller

Dick Chant gave me a 'wrap' when I won a double at the Cairns Amateur meeting with Quran and Grenoble Boy. 'Brian Mayfield-Smith is a very promising young trainer and I'm sure we're going to hear a lot more of him in the future,' he said. For the old man . . . that sort of acknowledgment swelled him right up.

* * *

When I got into strife at the Gordonvale State School and was threatened with expulsion (one of my mother's worst nightmares for her kids), my mum really blew up. She took me straight out of there. 'That's IT!' she said. Good, I thought, now I can go and do what I want to do—become a stockman. But my mum had other ideas. 'You won't be doing that,' she said. 'You're going to boarding school.'

My life changed when I was packed off to board at Charters Towers when I was thirteen. But the thing I liked best about my days at Mt Carmel was the sport. In my two years there, I managed to shine at cricket. I was an opening bowler with a bit of pace and I regularly used to get a fair swag of wickets in the inter-schools competition, Charters Towers having three boarding schools, plus the local high school. In fact two of my great memories of my years at Mt Carmel revolve around cricket. I remember as clear as yesterday listening on a scratchy old radio to the famous Australia–West Indies tied Test of 1961. The memory is so vivid that I can picture exactly the room I was in and where the radio was. And I remember everyone's disbelief when it came down to a tie late in the afternoon.

Then, even better, the great West Indian fast bowler Wes Hall came to Mt Carmel for a coaching clinic. As a fast bowler myself, I was rapt! One moment of that afternoon has always stayed in my mind: Wes Hall bowling to one of our First team batsmen on the number one oval. Hall, naturally, wasn't going at full tilt against a schoolboy player, but I can still see a ball he delivered that beat both the bat and the 'keeper—and ended up all the way down on the number two oval below.

I played rugby league too, as a wing three-quarter, although the game took something of a toll on me. In a tackle in my first year in the nine-stone (about fifty-seven kilograms) team, I broke a leg with an audible 'snap!'. The following year I broke a collarbone in a match against Charters Towers High. A bloke who was *very* big for an under-nine-stone team picked me up and speared me into the hard ground. I was taken by ambulance to Charters Towers Hospital and had to lie awkwardly all night with one arm dangling over the side of the bed.

In the morning a doctor came in and said, 'Get him out of bed and put him on a chair.' So they sat me on a chair, pulled my shoulders back, cross-bandaged me to hold my shoulder and hopefully pull the collarbone into place (the break being overlapping), put my arm in a sling and told me, 'You can go back to school now.'

Back there, I just had to poke along as best I could, putting up with the pain. After a week or two I became aware of a horrible smell; I had a look at my arm and could see this stuff oozing through the bandages. I went to the school matron and she carefully stripped the bandages off—and was shocked by what she saw. The bandage had cut into my armpit through the continual chafing since I'd been wearing it. It had been put on too tightly in the first place. Eventually it healed, with the proper care, but I've still got the scar today.

I remember a football match in the year I broke my leg. We were playing All Souls, a very competitive game in front of a big crowd. I made a run up the middle and when I was eventually tackled, another defender came crashing over the top just as I was getting up. My top teeth went straight through my bottom lip, sending blood spurting from my mouth. But I played on until eventually the sight of me must have been so off-putting that the referee said to me: 'You'd better go off and get that seen to.' I always remember that as I came through the gate, Bob Katter, later bound for fame as a National Party politician, called on the Mt Carmel contingent in the crowd to give 'Three cheers for Smithy!' I laugh about it now. Katter was a couple of grades ahead of me at Mt Carmel, and a real go-getter, even back then.

I got pretty used to discomfort in my early years. At Mt Carmel the pattern of me getting into trouble—and copping it as a result—continued. I was in the cadets and I seemed to spend a lot of time running around the oval with a .303 rifle raised above my head as punishment for some misdemeanour or omission.

I had friends at Mt Carmel, but I wasn't *real* close to anyone. People sort of tended to leave me alone a bit. I suppose I earned a bit of respect. One afternoon a bloke in a grade higher than me picked on me in front of a big group of blokes: 'I'll meet you behind the kitchen after study,' he challenged. Anyhow, a few of us went around, and I sorted him out even though he was a fair bit bigger than me. I was never that big; even in my twenties I was still only nine and a half stone (about sixty kilograms). I had a few blues like that at Mt Carmel, and eventually people sort of left me alone.

I never had any boxing tutoring. Mainly it was just determination. And I copped a flogging now and then over the years—you can't win them all. But as I said before, the physical hammering I copped in the 'interests' of discipline hardened me up, taught me how to handle things. Life is pretty soft for young people these days and, personally, I don't think it does anybody any harm to get a bit of a biff now and then.

✻ ✻ ✻

The best days of all were the holiday trips home, aboard a special train they'd put on from Charters Towers to Townsville, then heading on up the coast to Cairns. We used to have a ball on that train, the boys and girls from the different boarding schools mixing together, with kids dropping off at little stations all the way up the coast to go home to the family cane farm or cattle station. Going back to school on the same train, you'd feel like shit.

Life was full of simple pleasures for kids home on holidays in a country town like Cairns back in the fifties and early sixties. In that pre-television, pre-computer world, it was an outdoors life—the choice being the bush or the beach. The wonder of it was that as we climbed through the bush and tunnelled through the long grass, none of us ever got bitten by anything, although I can remember seeing deadly taipans at different times.

The beach was part of our lives in Cairns and from earliest days I can recall going to Yorkey's Knob and to Ellis Beach and Palm Beach with Mum and Dad and Lawrence after my father had finished work of an afternoon. Sharks were never a worry for us—there is a lot of shallow water around Cairns, a town built on an inlet—but awareness of the stingers that can kill you in almost an instant grew, particularly after a terrible event at a Cairns beach involving one of the brothers from Mt Carmel. In town on a holiday with some of the other staff, Brother Broderick, one of my teachers, emerged from the water with one of these stingers draped over his head and down his shoulders. He ran from the water screaming in pain, and they reckon he was dead within five minutes.

A great thrill for all the youngsters of the district was the arrival of Wirth's Circus in Gordonvale, something that happened each year between my fifth and eighth years. The circus would come to town by train, the animals packed on board. Something that has always stuck in my mind was an afternoon at the circus with my grandfather. As we left the big tent at the end of the show, we walked close to an elephant hitched to a cart. As we passed him, his big trunk came wavering down towards me—and I gave the elephant a Mintie. I'll never forget how gently he took it from me.

Probably even way back then a pattern was developing in my life. Some people who have difficulty relating to other people turn to animals as a refuge, as an alternative. So it was with me—and that reality shaped a lot of the attitudes I have held through my life. I have always had a deep love of animals, and for years now I have had a great sense of outrage at the injustices done to them.

My feeling for animals probably has had a fair bit to do with my success as a horse trainer. Even when I was at the top of the tree in the training business, I never looked at a horse as a commodity or a number. To me, they have always been an animal first, each one an individual, and I have treated them that way—not that I haven't done my block at times with horses, or dogs. We've probably all done that.

Once you get to know a bit about horses, you realise they're all very different, totally individual. A lot of people seeing a big mob of horses would see them as all pretty much the same, but when you know them, you can pick each one from a long way off. You get to recognise them by association, and by how they move. Just as you can recognise a person by the way he or she walks, so you can a horse.

CHAPTER FOUR

Wild Days Up North

On the night I left Mt Carmel College for the last time, a beautiful full moon rose to illuminate the train trip down to the coast. I remember sitting there elated, looking at the moon out of the carriage window and thinking, that's it! That's the end of school. I had battled through to the end of Year 10, a scholar of no great distinction. It was my mother who pushed me even that far, determined that I'd at least get a decent education. Later she said to me: 'Well, we've done all we can for you; we can't do any more.' My main thoughts on the train trip that night were that the years of heavy discipline and confinement were at last over.

In fact, they weren't . . .

Instead, my mother and father were quite adamant about me getting a trade. It wasn't what I wanted to do but, because they had worked hard to get me a 'good education', I reckoned I'd better go along with their wishes. So it came about that I started with an electrical contractor, George

Dalziel, who had a business in the next suburb, Freshwater. He was a good guy, George, and a terrific boss.

George and I shared a love of cricket and we played together in Sunday picnic matches at Freshwater. I was only a boy playing against the men, and these were pretty serious games, featuring some darned good cricketers. Probably, and not surprisingly, I had modelled myself on Wes Hall and would take this huge long run, then try to send them down as fast as I possibly could. One afternoon one of the older blokes pulled me aside with the words: 'Your run-up is too long—you're wearing yourself out. Take a shorter run-up and you'll last longer.' I must have had some ability. I was just a kid in a team of men, but they put up with me.

It was great working for George Dalziel. The only problem was, I had to go to night school twice a week and also back to day school, Cairns High, now and then, to work through the technical side of my apprenticeship. All of a sudden I was back to school days: I was being taught by guys who were teachers at the high school, and I had a couple of clashes with some of them. Then I found out that if you were pulled up before the Apprenticeship Board in Cairns three times, your indentures were automatically cancelled. I engineered that without too much trouble, so after about fourteen months as an apprentice electrician, I got my swag together, packed some gear—and headed west.

'Look, Mum, don't worry about me,' I'd said to my mother. 'I know you've done your best for me, but this is what I've always wanted to do. If I end up no good . . . well, it's not your fault.' I was sixteen.

✖✖✖

By answering an advertisement in *Country Life* I ended up getting my first job as a jackeroo on a cattle station called

Lake Vermont near the town of Claremont, west of Rockhampton. On the trip down to Rockhampton I talked with a couple of girls also travelling on the train. I was thinking to myself, jeeze, there won't be too much of this any more when I get out into the bush. There won't be too many girls out there.

I was still thinking those sorts of things as I stood alone on the railway station at Rocky, waiting to catch the Red Rattler west to Claremont. The Rattler was a cattle train with a carriage tacked on the back for the human cargo. It was a long, slow haul; we got to Claremont just on sun-up, and it was freezing bloody cold. There was a bloke from Dalgety's waiting for me at the station. (They were the stock and station agents who had organised the job.)

'The mail truck doesn't go until one o'clock this afternoon,' he told me. 'You'll just have to make your own amusement in the meantime—but I can tell you, there's not much to do here.' There wasn't—it was bloody boring—but eventually I met the mail truck bloke, hopped aboard, and off we went.

His job was to deliver mail and supplies to all the stations in the district. My job was to open and close all the gates—and there must have been 150 of them. It was one o'clock the next morning before we finally drove through the gates of Lake Vermont Station, last stop on the line. The bloke who ran the station had waited up for me and showed me to a room, already occupied by another young bloke. There were a couple of chain-wire beds, thin mattresses and two fairly light blankets. It was so cold I slept with my high-heeled boots and all my clothes on. I lay there for the rest of that first night wondering, and shivering, the bed squeaking from the movement. It was the winter of 1964.

By the time I got out there into the bush, I was a pretty good rider. It seemed there had always been horses in my life, ever since those very early days in Innisfail. Of course, people near us in Cairns had horses, and there always seemed to be the chance for me to go riding with a mate or two, down to the river. I wasn't brilliant, and I suppose that's pretty typical of me. There are a few things I'm pretty good at, but not brilliant. At Lake Vermont, though, I always got the job done—the job being a variety of things, like rounding up cattle, milking the cows and fixing fences.

It was a big station, some 400 square miles (nearly 650 square kilometres), although this was tiny compared to some of the Northern Territory stations I worked on later, notably Victoria River Downs, which was 5000 square miles (over 8000 square kilometres)—bigger than some countries.

The time at Claremont was the beginning of a great adventure in my life. Basically I just knocked around. I revelled in the freedom—the chance to roll my swag if I wished, hitch a ride or jump a train and go on to the next town. There were occasional dramas along the way. After I left Lake Vermont with one of the other blokes who worked there, we took jobs at a station further out. We travelled in one of those old Land Rovers through heavy rain (it was the rainy season) and somewhere out on the black cotton soil we got bogged, up to the mudguards. We were stranded for a day and a half before someone got through and took us to the nearest station. I have never been so hungry in my life as I was then. I was bloody starving.

The cattle station we ended up working for at that time was owned by the Barnes family, the people who had raced the champion stayer Tails. I wasn't interested in racing at all then. I was just interested in horses.

To kill time at the end of the cattle mustering season, I took a job on a sheep station near Hughenden. I don't much like sheep and had never worked with them, but I figured I had to do something. One of my main tasks there turned out to be plucking the wool off dead sheep—sheep that were blown up and green. That's how hungry that particular family of sheep farmers was. At the end of the day the owner would come along in his Holden ute to fetch me and the wool, a big bale on the back. It was bloody terrible work. The season was dry and the sheep would get bogged near the bore drain and be unable to get back. The crows would peck their eyes out while they were still alive.

The property was run by a father and son. One time the son headed off with his mother to another place they owned near Muttaburra, leaving me and the old man behind. Now and then we'd go out and shoot a kangaroo, as meat for the dogs. He'd hang it by a piece of eight-gauge wire to a big hook in the shed and would slice a piece off for the dogs at mealtime. One night he cooked dinner, a stew, and afterwards he asked, 'Did you enjoy that?'

'Yeah, it wasn't bad,' I said.

'Well,' he said, 'that was part of the roo leg from out in the shed.'

I don't think the Health Department would have been too impressed by the hygiene of that. I wasn't too impressed myself. But even though his cooking ethics left a bit to be desired, he gave me a piece of valuable advice that I never forgot. 'Son,' he said, 'you'll only get a few real opportunities in life. Learn to recognise them—and don't let them pass you by.'

⁂

Later, I went to Kamilaroi Station, 150 miles (about 240 kilometres) or so along a dirt road north of Cloncurry, a big place owned by Australian Estates. They had half a dozen stations in the area, and this was one of them. When I arrived at the town of Cloncurry, I stayed at the Queen's Hotel, run by a very nice woman named Shirley Anderson. When I contacted the station on arrival, they told me there wouldn't be a truck heading out there for another five or six days. That's great, I thought. The thing was, I had got to Cloncurry on a wing and a prayer. I had about £20 in my pocket, and that was all I had in the world.

The first few days there, I had a couple of drinks, but I wasn't eating much at all. Then Shirley came up to my room. 'How come you're not coming to meals?' she asked.

'Oh, I'm not really hungry,' I told her.

She just looked at me. 'You haven't got any money, have you?' she said.

'Yeah, I've got a bit . . . I can pay for the room,' I said.

'That's not what I meant,' she said. 'When are they coming to pick you up?' I told her it would be a few days yet. 'Look, you just get your meals, whatever you want,' she said. 'You can pay me back out of your first month's pay.'

Thanks to Shirley Anderson's kindness, I was right after that. A couple of nights later, another ringer bloke and I were in the bar, as pissed as parrots. Around the other side were a couple of town blokes with a radio, listening to the Lionel Rose–Fighting Harada World Bantamweight Title fight from Tokyo, well after the pub's 11.00 p.m. closing time. I was full of piss and I said to one of the blokes, 'I'll bet you £20 Rose wins.'

'I'll take the bet,' said one of them, although he added some derogatory words about the Japanese fighter. Politically incorrect talk was a fact of life back then. Anyhow, Rose won—and the bloke paid me. 'Do you know who that bloke was last night?' the barman asked me the next day.

'No idea,' I said.

'He's a local cop,' said the barman. We'd all been breaking

the law, of course, but in country towns that's just the way it was.

I finally got to Kamilaroi, and stayed a year or so. Life was pretty basic, but I enjoyed it. When we were at the out-station itself, Mullala, we lived in a house they had built there, sleeping under mosquito nets in beds on the verandah. Only the head stockman had his own bedroom. Then, when we went out mustering, we would camp at night on the ground in our swags at a place close to the mustering circuit stockyards. If it rained . . . well, you got rained on. We would muster all the country around those stockyards, bringing the cattle in daily, branding and drafting, and generally cleaning up the area before moving on to the next camp. There we'd do the same thing, before moving on again. The full circuit took almost half a year.

✖✖✖

I worked at Victoria River Downs in the Northern Territory. When I was there it had an estimated 70,000 head of cattle on it, and very few fences. Fifty thousand of the 70,000 were cleanskins, meaning wild cattle. We would ride on a mob of cattle during the day—there might be 2000 head of them—and they'd take off just like any other wild animals. In the afternoon we might get back to camp with 300 of them. The rest would have gotten away. If you were mustering upwind of them, you'd never see them, because they would get your scent. All you would ever see were tracks on the ground, and fresh shit. On the station was the main stock camp, then an outlying camp called Moolooloo, forty miles (about sixty-five kilometres) away, then two others, Mt Sanford and Pigeon Hole. I was sent to Moolooloo.

We could be out in the bush for months at a time and all we'd have would be our swags, which consisted of a canvas with about four blankets rolled in it, one change of clothes, soap, tobacco, toothpaste, a towel—and that was it. All our gear was strapped onto packhorses and mules, and you had to try to keep the bulk down. There was a standing joke that if someone had too big a swag he had a 'married man's swag'. We travelled light, living off corned beef, tinned peas and beans—stuff that was portable. No fresh fruit or veggies, of course.

There is something of an art to working cattle. They are all different to work, depending on the type of country they are running on. It's not just a matter of finding them, hunting them up and drafting them. At the beginning of a muster the first thing that would happen was that they would bring in the horses, about seventy in all. They would have been out in the bush during the wet season, and they'd be pretty fiery because they hadn't been ridden for months. As they were drafted through the yards the head stockman would say, 'That's yours . . . that's yours . . .' We'd get four each and would have to rough each horse out, and shoe it. They were pretty wild; they'd buck like hell and you'd have to ride them until they settled and got the bush wildness out of them. After about a week the camp was ready to go mustering, and you'd rotate your horses so they'd work once every four days, maybe only half a day if it was very rough country.

Inevitably a lot of them would still have the wildness in them, and they'd buck to try to get rid of you. On an early morning in winter you'd be freezing, and you'd grab the saddle . . . The horse would be looking at you with the whites of his eyes, and he'd half hump up as you were doing up the girth, showing he was going to explode. You'd lead him for a bit, but he still wouldn't relax, so you'd swing on and, next thing you'd know, he'd let out a bit of a snort and a roar and then you'd be hanging on for dear life. After a while he'd get it out of his system and settle. Only then could you go to work.

Mustering was from March to November. From November onwards it got too hot, and later on the rainy season would come. After the rains there would be a lot of green grass around and a *lot* of flies. If you happened to be in camp then, it was a real battle. The camp food was basic—stew or meat, or the cook might make a bit of savoury mince—and you'd get your food on a tin plate, then find a spot to sit down. By the time you did, everything you had in your hand would be covered in flies. You'd be waving them away, trying to grab a mouthful, but they'd just come swarming back.

For all those sorts of minor and major hardships, I loved the adventure of it. As far as I was concerned, the harder a horse bucked, the better. If I got on and the horse only sort of crow-hopped . . . well, I was disappointed. You'd test yourself out, show off a bit in front of the others. We used to get twenty-four quid ($48) a week and we'd work seven days a week for that, with an occasional Sunday off. There's not much to do in a stock camp *except* work, considering that you haven't even got a bed, let alone a room. If you were just going to sit around under a tree on your swag all day and read a book, it would get very boring.

***

Characters abounded. Some of the funniest ones were certainly the camp cooks, a strange and cranky lot in my experience. Generally, they seemed to be raging alcoholics. There was one I recall who, when he was putting in the camp food order, would include a massive requisition for vanilla essence. From that he could make some sort of potent brew. More than once we came back to camp after mustering to find him flaked out, drunk as a skunk, under his fly tent and we'd have to rustle up dinner ourselves. It was tolerated to a point, because cooks weren't that easy to find.

I recall another bloke who never mixed with the stockmen. He did his job cooking the meals, then he'd go back into his tent and read a book. One night we were back from mustering, sitting around the fire on our haunches smoking and talking—mostly rubbish—and he came out and made a stew in the camp oven. We were talking away and he went back to his tent for a while. Then he came out again. 'Tea's on,' he said. No one moved—we were yarning about something—so he went back to his tent and read a few more pages of his book. Then he appeared again, quietly picked up the pot and poured the stew out on the ground. 'Tea's off,' he said. What the hell??? On subsequent nights whenever he said, 'Tea's on', everyone jumped to attention.

* * *

It was a unique lifestyle, as remote from the lives most people lead as being on another planet. In the towns in those times there's no doubt that the stockmen and ringers were looked on as no-hopers. I remember being up early in Cloncurry one morning and out in the street in my jeans, a ringer's shirt, a hat and high-heeled boots. There weren't many people around but a woman came past with a little girl. 'Look, Mummy . . . look at the cowboy,' said the kid.

The woman grabbed her hand. 'You come away now,' she said.

And that's how it was.

There was drinking and gambling and fighting. I suppose 'colourful' is a word that gets pretty close to the mark. I had many experiences, some of them a little vague due to the alcohol haze I was in during them. I remember hopping in a ute with a couple of other young ringers one day and driving up to the Gregory races, right up in the Gulf Country above Kamilaroi Station. It was a typical bush race meeting. Everyone was on the drink. From what I remember of Gregory, it consisted of a pub, a racecourse, a town hall, a church and a shop. That was about it.

After the races it was back to the town pub. I recall a little poddy foal walking into the bar one night. He was owned by the publican, so there were no problems—in fact the bloke gave the foal a stubby of beer, which he downed like an old stager.

Meanwhile, one of the bookies from the races had set up a Crown & Anchor gaming table and everyone was into it. I ended up winning a few hundred quid at which point I declared: 'That's it. I've got mine—and I'm not going to give any of it back.'

Anyhow, I got on the piss with a couple of blokes in the bar and after a time I pulled a £20 note out. 'I'll just go and give this a try,' I said. 'When it's gone I'll be straight back.' You might have guessed the ending—I ended up losing everything I had won, plus the extra £20 I had pulled out. It was a pretty fair lesson for me on the subject of gambling.

As the night wore on we all ended up out the front of the pub, sitting on the grass under a tree. The foal was still wandering around and people were giving him beers which he kept downing. Everyone thought that was very amusing. Finally he was so pissed he fell over, and was just lying there. He made a bit of an attempt to get up, lifting his head and neck, but then he sort of groaned, like 'Oh, stuff it!', and his head went down and he went to sleep. Soon another one of the drunks had flaked out, using the little horse's stomach as a cushion. That's where we all slept, out there on the ground under the stars.

What woke me in the morning—apart from the flies swarming all over me—was a noise, a clink, clink, clink I could hear. Anyway, when I finally came to and pulled myself up, there was the little foal, pawing at the empty stubbies, looking for another drink. He was just like a hungover human being, looking for a hair of the dog. Oh jeeze, I thought, this could only happen up here.

At Kamilaroi Station, they didn't pay overtime—none of them did in those days. Instead, all the stockmen would get a week's break in town to make up for the overtime they had worked. There was method in the management's madness. They knew we'd go to town, blow all our money—and have to come back to work to earn some more. And that's what would happen in those wild weeks. We'd get drunk and bet and fight, and at the end of the week a truck from the station would come to town and do the rounds of the Cloncurry pubs. They'd drag us out, throw us in the vehicle and take us back to work.

I especially remember one occasion, involving me and the head stockman in camp at that time, a big bloke named Ron Amy who used to wear a ten-gallon hat. After our week in town the round-up had taken place and we were on our way back to Kamilaroi. About sixty-five kilometres out of Cloncurry there is a little siding called Quamby, a cattle-loading place which back then had a pub, a few houses, a tiny school and not much else. We were all pretty drunk anyway, but we decided we'd pull up there and get stuck into some more. I remember lying on my swag in the back of the truck after we left the Quamby pub, and watching over the side as we almost wiped out a bloke on a pushbike. Then someone yelled: 'Pull up, pull up! I want a piss.'

There were about seven of us, standing in a row alongside the truck, having a piss. I happened to be standing alongside Ron Amy and somehow or other we started having words. 'I never liked you, anyway,' he said to me.

'Well, you're just a big bag of shit,' I replied.

The insults continued—we were both mad drunk—and next thing we were shaping up. I was still only about nine and a half stone dripping wet, and Ron was a big lump of a fella, even taller via the high-heeled riding boots he was sporting.

I'll just keep jabbing him, I thought to myself. I won't let him get near me. So I kept hitting him, and managing to evade his swings, until eventually Jimmy Stevens, the camp cook, said to Ron: 'Let him go, old fella. He's too quick for you . . . you're too big and slow.'

We jumped back into the truck, and finally made it to the main station. As soon as we got there, though, a blue was on again, with me in it. Eventually, when it settled a bit, we got back into the truck and headed the extra sixty-five kilometres to the outstation. There the drinking started again around the campfire—and all of a sudden there was another blue. So that was it—three blues in the one day, and with three different blokes.

After we got back from town the drinking would generally last for about three days and the management would let it go. Then Jimmy Mitchell, the manager at Kamilaroi, a bloke who could drink a bit of rum himself, would come out to the camp. 'Right, this is what you've got to do,' he'd say. He knew how long to leave us alone. Once we got it out of our system, we'd be back into the work and we'd always brand more calves and finish before the team at the main station camp. That was just how things operated out there.

The rule was that there was no grog in camp. The only time we had a drink in camp was when we brought some back from the breaks in town. Once that was all drunk, that was the end of it. Any 'sneak' drinking in camp meant the sack for sure. They were the rules.

There was a Saturday afternoon when we were in Cloncurry, drinking at the Post Office Hotel. The pub was owned by a bloke named Baldy Chapman who had Boomerah, the station next to Kamilaroi. Baldy had a big claim to fame: he had been the owner of a horse named Bore Head when it won the Caulfield Cup in a photo finish in 1965. In the pub then (and maybe now) was a big photograph of the finish and down on the rails there's a bald-headed bloke with his hat raised high in the air. All the locals used to reckon that was Baldy Chapman.

Anyhow, on this Saturday arvo the races were on the radio—of course—and I was playing darts with a couple of other young ringers. I got up to have my turn and when I got back to the bar, my stool was gone. 'Where's my stool?' I said to one of my mates.

'He took it,' he said, indicating a big, heavyset bloke in a PMG outfit, drinking with a couple of other blokes.

I'm going to look pretty weak if I let him get away with that, I thought, so I walked over and tapped him on the shoulder. 'Mate, you've got my stool,' I said.

'What are you talking about?' he answered.

'I'm talking about you knocking my stool off while I was having my shot at darts,' I said.

With that, he pushed me. 'Get away,' he said. So, I just let him have it—with a straight left. He sort of blinked and said, 'Look, if you don't nick off, I'll pull your head off!'

'Mate, you never sucked the milk,' I said, hoping that insulting his mother would get things lively.

'Okay—out the back,' said the big bloke.

The whole bar was suddenly galvanised into movement and everyone poured out into the yard behind the pub—a pretty typical space, gravelly and with a clothesline wandering across it. 'I'll back the ringer,' someone shouted. The girls who worked in the pub all had their heads poked out the windows at the commotion.

Anyhow, we were into it—and he started throwing them like a windmill. I figured that the only way I was going to beat him was to keep hitting him with straight lefts and keep moving away from him. Which I kept doing, and through the haze one of them caught him quite nicely. His head snapped back, and the blood started coming out of his nose. I thought, this is my chance, and skipped in and whacked him straight under the breastbone, which usually curls them up. He went down and was sort of kneeling, leaning up against the clothesline. I grabbed him by the collar and pulled his head around and hit him again.

'I've had enough,' he said.

'No you haven't,' I said. 'I'll give you another one.' At that point the mob intervened. 'Come on, he's had enough, leave him alone.' I reckoned I'd proved my point anyway.

So we all headed back into the pub and resumed the darts and the drinking and the yarning. And I got my stool back. All was forgotten. After a while the big bloke came over to me. 'Where do you come from, anyway?' he asked.

'I'm from Cairns,' I said.

'Oh, I'm from up that way m'self,' he said.

There was an element of fair play about scraps back then. There was one line of thought that my instincts told me to follow—that if you knocked someone down, you let them get up and have another go. But the other overriding thought which made more sense was that if someone went down, then you'd bloody well better keep them down—otherwise they might get up and give you a hiding. Putting in the boot was never part of fights then. I certainly never subscribed to it.

There came a time when the adventure started to wear

off for me. I'd look around at the other ringers and I'd think, is this going to be me when I'm fifty? There were some crazy things went on out there, I can tell you. In the times we weren't working there was a hell of a lot of OP rum consumed, and blokes would sort of go into the horrors. I remember one night sitting with some of the others in a circle out on the back verandah at Kamilaroi and this silly old bugger came out, full of rum and brandishing a pistol. He fired it off into the concrete floor and fragments flew everywhere, one of them hitting me in the neck and drawing blood. I've still got the mark.

In telling these stories now I'm only trying to paint a genuine picture of what it was like. I'm not so proud of some of the things that went on in my earlier life. But they happened.

* * *

I worked a total of five years as a stockman on various stations across outback Queensland and the Northern Territory. Working my way through Queensland stations Kamilaroi, Mt Surprise, Killarney (a sheep station), Lake Vermont and on to the vast, sprawling Victoria River Downs and Daly Waters stations in the Territory, I experienced a life that I suppose couldn't have been more 'Australian'.

Photos from the time generally show me astride a horse, a lean figure, inevitably sporting a wide-brimmed hat which I swapped in later years for a city-style Stetson. At the schools I attended, a hat was a required part of the uniform, and I've pretty much worn one ever since. For practical reasons I wore a hat in the years when I was a ringer on outback cattle stations in the heat of North Queensland and the Northern Territory. Later, when I became a horse trainer, it seemed to me that . . . well, a hat was the *trademark* of a trainer, and I should wear one. As the racing years went by, I suppose it became my own trademark. People think of me as the bloke in the hat and recognise me at the racecourse for that. I'm comfortable with it. I think you can probably put me down as being on the tail end of the old school—those days when every man wore a hat. Anyway, I looked a real 'bushie' back then, and I have always seen myself that way, at heart. In 1987, I told a Sydney racing journalist, 'I wouldn't live in the city for a week if I wasn't successful at this caper [horse training].'

In the early months and years in these faraway places I pretty much thought that this would be it for me in my working life. After all, there were blokes out there on the stations who were lifetime ringers and stockmen, blokes in their late fifties who had done nothing else. I remember an old drover on Lorraine Station—Paddy, with his white hair and beard. I struck him up there one time when he was doing contract mustering. What happens with mustering is that when you're on a station and you're mustering near the border or boundary of an adjoining station, they invite you to come across to identify and retrieve those of your boss's cattle that have got through the fences. This particular year the mustering had started, but the rainy season hadn't quite finished. An old hand, Paddy had his ancient truck at the campsite, with a fly tent over his bed. Also with him was his daughter, an attractive girl in her twenties who was our cook and who used to wear shorts around the place. She was, in fact, quite a distraction for the guys.

It had rained hard and late that year, and was still raining when we camped between a creek on one side, and a river on the other. The creek filled and overflowed and the water was running across to the river—via our camp. For quite a time Paddy and his daughter tried desperately to hold back the tide, building a dirt wall, determined to keep their spot dry. Inevitably, the water won, as it usually does . . . and under it all went. I can still see the moment when Paddy threw his arms in the air. 'Fuck it!' he exclaimed. 'Let's go musterin'.'

***

The Northern Territory stations mix white and black stockmen, and in my experience it worked well. In the stock camps where I worked, there would be a white head stockman, three other white stockmen, and eight or ten Aboriginal stockmen. The Aboriginal blokes generally had their own little camp, where they could talk their tribal language, and we had ours. They seemed happy with their own company, and there was no abuse of anyone because of colour, no real dramas. We respected their abilities, and what they could do. The best of them were quite fearless and loved nothing better than showing how they could ride a rough horse, or throw a wild bull.

It's fair to say, though, that it's no easy thing when you're stuck out in the bush in a small group for weeks—or months—at a time. People start to get on each other's nerves, and I admit I had a fair bit of difficulty with that reality at times. Small things that people do gradually become big irritations. You get sick of people, and when they irritate you, you take it as an affront. Things can go downhill from there. Increasingly I would get the feeling that my privacy and my space were being invaded too much, and I would resent the intrusion. Yeah, camp life could be very difficult and by the time the chance of a break came in the off-season, you'd need it. Desperately. Those years toughened me, though. Out there was no place for wimps. It taught you to be a man in pressure situations. It was a hard life . . . very lonely at times.

I remember having my twenty-first birthday at Kamilaroi Station in the Gulf. There was no celebration. Mr parents had bought me a record player which they sent up to Kamilaroi. On the day, I set it up in my room at the ringers' quarters and listened to Marty Robbins' gunfighter ballads, and to a Slim Dusty LP. I felt very alone—and lonely.

Some bloody twenty-first birthday, this, I thought to myself as I lay there on the bed.

Sometimes when the wet season came, I would go back to the coast, to Cairns. But if I was short of money I might stay on at a station, working through the wet doing odd jobs, maintenance jobs that needed to be done—fixing fences, repairing windmills.

I can't remember the exact moment when I decided I'd seen enough of that sort of life, done enough. I had always had a bit of ambition in me anyway—I had ideas to be someone, to make something of my life. I would dream about getting a bit of ground for myself one day, maybe even a station of my own, or at least becoming manager of a station. There began a period during which, more and more, I would look at the blokes around me and think, this is a pretty bloody futile life—I really don't want to finish up like you guys. Some of them were drunks and no-hopers. The pattern of the passing years for some of them was no more than this: work hard and get drunk. All your life.

* * *

In 1968, I came in from the bush during the off-season and took a job at the big meatworks in Cairns. With no great enthusiasm, I took with me an expectation that I would probably return from there to work once more on one of the outback cattle stations. The job in the meatworks was certainly no great distraction to any future plans I might have—a lowly position in the salt hides shed.

But the job was a brief interlude that changed my life. One afternoon during a smoko, I was sitting out the back with a few of the guys. The subject was horseracing—something I'd never taken much interest in—and they were talking about strappers. There was a good old bloke there named Alf Eales, and I asked him: 'What's a strapper?' He explained it was a stablehand who looked after racehorses. Hmm. I sat there thinking that maybe if I could get into that line of work, I'd still be working with horses, and I might be able to make a go of that business.

'How d'you get into it?' I asked Alf after a while.

'Well, you've just got to go and get a job in a stable,' said Alf. 'But you won't get a start here [in Cairns]. They generally just do it themselves, or have someone from the family involved.' As the conversation went to and fro, someone mentioned a trainer they knew of in Brisbane: Tony Mazzaglia, of Hendra.

CHAPTER FIVE

Animal Encounters

Right through my life I've had some hair-raising experiences with animals. Twice in earlier days up north, close encounters I had with animals could easily have brought a swift and premature end to my life. Needing a little bit of luck on both occasions, I survived to tell the stories.

Mustering wild cattle always had an edge of danger to it. What we often had to do was target bulls in the herd, because when they came to the 'boundary' of their run, they'd lead other cattle away and break out the mob. We stockmen would wear bull straps around our stomachs, and would single out the bulls to chase. When they started to tire, their hindquarters would begin to roll, and at that point you'd jump off your horse and grab the bull by the tail. When he swung around to hook you, you'd have him off-balance, and he would lose his hind end and fall. By then you'd have the bull strap in your teeth and you'd quickly wrap it around the two back legs, immobilising the bull. Cattle are different to horses in that they always get up from the ground rear end first, so if you have the back legs immobilised, they can't get up. When you had the bull down and strapped, the rest of the stock would be brought along—it might be 300 head or so of quiet cattle, which they called 'coachers', and eventually you'd take the strap off and the bull would run into the mob. And that's how you'd try to get them back to camp.

One afternoon on Victoria Downs we were heading back to camp with a big mob of cattle, making our way across a high rocky plateau which fell away down to a creek. At the water's edge I spotted a cleanskin bull, a real big fella, and I broke away and chased after him on my own. He headed along the cattle pad beside the creek as fast as he could go, with me after him at full gallop. When he tired, I picked the moment and the spot, jumped off, and grabbed him by the tail. The problem was, he had shit on his tail and my hands slipped. I managed to pull him down, but when I went to flank him I was too slow, because I couldn't get a proper grip, and in an instant he hit his legs again. At that point, I was in big trouble . . .

I did the only thing I could do—I grabbed his tail as short as I could, and hung on for dear life. He kept spinning around, trying to get rid of me, and I was bouncing off rocks one second, scraping along the ground the next. The pain was excruciating as I bounced across the terrain, but I wouldn't let go. I knew if I did, he would kill me. He was a big, fully grown bull with a thick neck and big, heavy horns.

Suddenly through all the haze and pain everything stopped. When I looked up he wasn't there—he was about thirty metres away. Two black stockmen who had seen me go after him had followed behind and, seeing my plight, had thrown rocks at the bull and he'd sort of half-charged them.

They distracted him just long enough for me to climb up into the fork of a dead tree that was stuck in the rocks nearby, its roots sort of entwined in the rocks. There was one big solid fork in it no higher than about two metres off the ground, but it was just high enough.

The bull turned and ran back to me. I was tucked up in the tree in my high-heeled boots and spurs, my legs curled up just out of his reach, and he was underneath, snorting and trying to hook me out. All he had to do was lean on the tree and it would have fallen, for sure. It was just propped up precariously between the rocks. Thankfully, he didn't think of that. He hung around for a while and then obviously thought, ah, bugger you, and wandered off along the cattle pad and out of sight.

Finally I got down out of the tree and the Aboriginal guys retrieved my horse and came across. 'Are you okay?' they asked.

'Yeah, I'm bloody sore, but I'm fine, thanks,' I answered.

I got back on my horse, and fortunately we only had to ride up the ridge and cross a river and we were back in camp. Halfway up the ridge the delayed shock hit. I started to dry retch, and my whole body began to shake uncontrollably.

It was wintertime, with sharp, cold nights that closed in quickly, and that night I lay in my swag under four blankets and a canvas cover, shivering, sore and bloody miserable. It was one of the most wretched nights I have ever spent as I thought how close I had come to death, really thought about the sort of danger I had been in. If the other stockmen hadn't come along, or if I had let go of the tail earlier, I would have been a goner. He would have got me, for sure. What wild cattle do is, if they can't get you with their horns they just kneel on you with their brisket—and crush you that way.

The next day, because it is expected of you that you can't be a softie or a sissy, I had to get up and go and do my job like nothing had happened. But I can say now that every move was agony.

It was the closest call I had while droving, although a fall from a horse one day when he stepped in a crack in the black cotton soil and rolled over on me, pinning one of my legs against a rock, had me in plenty of trouble too. When he finally rolled away I could barely get up, let alone walk. I was out on my own, at Victoria River Downs, and a fair way from camp. I thought, jeeze, this is lovely . . . no one knows where I am. I went and sat under a tree and held onto the horse for a couple of hours. Eventually I managed to drag myself back into the saddle, using my 'good' leg, and made it back. But I had badly ripped muscles in the groin and couldn't ride for four or five days after that. The interesting thing is that years later, when we were going to Africa, Maree and I had a medical examination at St Vincent's Hospital, during which they check everything it's possible to check. When they did a scan on my groin, they found a lump. That'd be bloody right, I thought. I'm ready to go to Africa, and I've got cancer or something. Anyhow, it turned out that I had a gland in the groin which had turned fibrous and gone hard. I thought back to the day the horse pinned me against a rock, remembering the pain and discomfort, and wondered whether that was behind it.

My second brush with death came several years after my confrontation with the cleanskin bull, in my very early days as a horse trainer in Cairns. A fractious filly named Gay Meld, who in all other ways was very good to me, almost drowned me in the Mulgrave River one morning. Gay Meld, in fact, was my first winner as a trainer, bolting in at Mareeba one Saturday in 1971 to kick-start my career.

Throughout her career, she was always a nervy horse, and would often stir up. One day I took her out to a place they called the Green Patch, on the Mulgrave River at Gordonvale.

There was no-one else in the stable in those days, just me, so my mother came along to help.

I would always swim with my horses back then and I was in the water with Gay Meld that day, an exercise which involved floating along beside the horse, gently guiding it by the reins, with any weight pressure taken by a short hold on the mane, just forward of the wither—when something frightened her. She panicked. Her head went up, and her eyes were rolling with fear, then she went right off, thrashing wildly. I was just doing what I could to stay out of the way, hanging onto the reins without trying to pull her around, when I felt something hook me in the right thigh and drag me under the water . . .

All of a sudden I was being thrown around well under the waters of the Mulgrave, and with this painful, grabbing sensation in my thigh. I was struggling desperately to get back up, but just couldn't get clear, and I started to see red and black. My ears were ringing and my chest was becoming tighter and tighter. Suddenly, and not a moment too soon, I was free, shooting to the surface where I gasped in the air in great gulps.

What had happened was this: in her terrified thrashing around, the filly had kicked me and the back of the shoe had hooked into my leg, right up to the back nail. I had only got free when the skin on my leg had ripped away. When I lifted my leg in the water to see what had happened, I could see the damage that had been done. My mother had watched the whole thing from the river bank. I was wearing a hat, as usual, and when the trouble started all she could see was the horse going berserk, and my hat bobbing furiously in the churning water. There was no sign of me, so you can imagine how my mum was feeling.

Eventually I got to the bank with the horse. 'Are you all right? Are you all right?' asked my mother.

'Yeah, I'm fine, I just cut my leg a little bit,' I said, with some bravado. In fact my leg was laid open; it wasn't bleeding much, but it looked terrible. My mum, who had been a nurse, took one look and promptly declared: 'That's bad—you'll have to have a skin graft. You could pick up anything in this river.' She was always scared of tetanus. 'You won't be able to take the horse back to Cairns; you'll have to go straight to a doctor.'

'Well, I can't just leave her here,' I said. I waited by the river while she headed off as quickly as she could to round up Bert Healey, an old trainer we knew from Gordonvale. Bert helped load the filly into the float, and then Mum and he took me to the ambulance station in Gordonvale. From there I was conveyed to Cairns Base Hospital.

They stitched me and bandaged me, and I went back to the stables that afternoon, the fact being there was no-one else to do the work. My leg was bloody sore, but in a one-man training operation, there wasn't a lot of choice but to keep going. The wound I had suffered healed over a period of weeks, but near it was a brown patch the size of a hand, which developed small sores. It wouldn't go away and, after a time, it started to ulcerate.

On my mother's advice I went to a skin specialist. He took a swab and later told me the bad news: 'You have an infection there that won't respond to drugs. You're going to have to have all that cut out—then you'll need a skin graft.'

'How long will that take?' I asked him.

'You could be laid up for a month . . . it could be longer,' said the doc.

'I can't do it,' I said. 'I've got eight horses in the stable, and I've got no-one to look after them.'

The doctor looked at me for a minute, then said: 'You make up your mind whether you want your eight horses . . . or your leg.'

So, there was no choice. I organised an old trainer from Cairns to come in and keep an eye on the horses, and asked Mum to keep an eye on *him*, the fact being that he was a bit of a drinker. Before long, I was flat on my back in Cairns Base Hospital, my mind ticking over endlessly.

They took strips of skin off the inside of one of my legs, and laid them on the wound. Luckily for me, the first graft 'took'. I was in hospital for four frustrating weeks. In the eleven years that followed, I never had a single day off.

Chapter Six

Travelling Man

Early one morning in 1967, I threw my swag into the back of my old Holden ute and headed south on the long trek to Brisbane. I got there, to Tony Mazzaglia's establishment in suburban Hendra, late on the afternoon of the next day. They were cleaning up the yard, and someone pointed out the boss. 'Have you got any jobs for strappers?' I asked him.

'Have you got any experience?' he responded.

'No,' I admitted, 'but I've been around horses all my life as a stockman.'

There was a pause and then he turned to one of the boys: 'is there a spare bed in the room?'

'Yeah,' came the answer.

'Bring your gear in,' said Mazzaglia. 'You can start now.'

I lasted just a few months, pretty much a fish out of water in the 'big' city, although they were good to me. Tony had about twenty horses and was renowned as an Albion Park specialist, the near-city track where they raced on sand. I never really felt at home—I hardly knew anyone, and I wasn't happy. Eventually I decided one day, bugger this—I'm going back to the bush. So I gave my notice, threw all my gear in the back of the ute and headed due northwest. I drove all the way through the back country to a place I knew, Cloncurry—a fair drive on my own. And from there I went further still, on to Kamilaroi Station and the resumption of my life as a stockman.

But there was a restlessness in me now, and I didn't last too long at Kamilaroi this time. I awoke one morning in my swag under an already burning sun, with the flies swarming, and I thought, this is not really my life any more . . . there must be something better. For me, the adventure was over. After a time, I heard of a job going at a thoroughbred stud out Toowoomba way, so I headed south again, and managed to get a start there, at the Zischke family's Panorama Stud at Allora. I thought that working on a horse stud might provide a happy medium, that maybe it would turn out to be the answer I was looking for.

Panorama Stud in fact proved an interesting experience, if not the end of my search. They had a couple of imported stallions there, Ballywit and Freestyle, and old Jack Zischke, who owned the place and who bred a lot of good horses over the years, said to me, 'What about if we get these two ready for the Brisbane Exhibition?' From that day the horses became my responsibility and I started feeding and working and lunging them to prepare for Queensland's biggest show of the year. To cut a long story short, the two of them went down to the show—and Ballywit emerged there as grand champion thoroughbred. The day after he was named, I ended up with my picture in the paper, the Brisbane *Courier Mail*, proudly leading Ballwyit around the ring.

✻ ✻ ✻

During my first, brief stay in the racing business, at Tony Mazzaglia's stable, I became pretty good mates with Tony Erhart, who was Brisbane's leading apprentice, and going so well back then he was also the leading jockey. At one stage Tony was campaigning with a couple of Mazzaglia horses in Sydney, Autumn Queen and Panwick. 'I'm going to fly you to Sydney,' Tony Mazzaglia said to me one day, 'and you can give Tony a hand to bring the two horses back in the float.'

Tony Erhart met me at Mascot airport and took me for a bit of a spin, across the Harbour Bridge and back, and up through Kings Cross—which was something of an eye-opener for a young bloke from the bush. We stayed that night, before the trip home, in a loft at stables run by George Musson at Rosehill, and when I left my job at Panorama Stud, it was to Sydney I headed, and to the only place I knew down there—the Musson Stables. The year was 1968.

I arrived in Sydney in peak hour, which is not much fun even when you know the city well, which I didn't. I headed in the general direction of Parramatta, finally got my bearings and reached George Musson's place late in the afternoon. 'Well, to tell you the truth I don't need anyone at the moment,' said George when I asked him the question. He was a real punting trainer, George. He'd wait and wait, then set one up and have a really good go. And he was pretty successful at that. Punting trainers generally end up with a sandshoe on one foot and a galosher on the other. 'Jack Denham down at Nebo Lodge is always looking for boys,' George went on. 'Go down and see him.'

So, at six o'clock that night I knocked on Jack Denham's back door. Denham himself answered, and I asked him whether he had any jobs going. 'Get your gear and take it over to the room there—and be on deck at four o'clock in the morning,' he said. So, with little fuss I became a strapper at Nebo Lodge, a place that was to play a big part in my future in racing, although of course this was unbeknown to me at the time.

✵✵✵

Strapping is a pretty bloody hard life. In those days, after the food money was taken out, you'd end up with about $30 a week. Every fortnight you'd get a 'weekend off'. However, the weekend off didn't start until you'd finished doing the horses late on the Sunday morning. Monday at 4.00 a.m. you'd be back on duty. I stayed with Denham about eighteen months and I suppose I learned a bit, although not too much. Denham, by then training for S & M Fox Investments never ventured much, and eventually I decided there wasn't much point asking him. I thought I'd just keep my eyes and ears open, and ask the right people now and then. I was always there on time, and where I had to be—I did my job well, and I was never bothered. But it was no great 'apprenticeship' or anything like that. When I look back on my time in racing, I have no doubt that most of what I have learned in the game has come about through trial and error, or through things I have gleaned for myself over the years.

Jack Denham had only been at Nebo Lodge about sixteen months when I went there. He had sixty horses in work and would get a fairly modest return of about four winners a month, three of them at the provincials, even though we had some well-bred horses. He was no leading trainer then, no guru to follow—and the truth of it is, I never had one of those. I never worked for Tommy Smith or Bart Cummings or Colin Hayes, and I look back over the long years and wonder how much better I could have been if I *had* worked for one of them. Sure, I worked for Tony Mazzaglia, a lovely bloke, but his horses mainly won only at Albion Park ('The

Creek') or at the provincials. And I learned a bit talking to Tony Erhart in my time there. Albert McKenna, who I also worked for in Sydney, only popped up with a winner every so often, and the Denham stable was certainly not in full swing when I worked there. In the learning stakes, I pretty much skimmed over the surface.

It took Denham about three years to get the hang of the whole thing and to get it going properly, and then he started to come out with his good horses and his successes in big races. That was twelve to eighteen months after I had left Nebo Lodge. In my experience, Denham would never tell you anything. If you asked him a question he would look at you as if you were asking for his last ten bob. The bloke I *did* learn from was Mick Denham, Jack's brother, who worked in the stable and was a very knowledgable horseman. The story was that Mick got outed and Jack took over the horses—and by the time Mick was allowed back in, Jack was the trainer and Mick had to settle for a lesser role.

✖ ✖ ✖

Even there, linked to a growing stable in a big city, I didn't feel as though I was getting anywhere in racing. From my $30 a week, I used to spend $18 taking an hour's flying lesson at the nearby Bankstown Airport. I have always had a love of flying; it's that freedom thing that has always been so important to me. Back then I was always searching for something, and I didn't really know what it was. After I left Denham's I got a job in the Goodyear Tyre Factory near Rosehill Racecourse, figuring I would try a different lifestyle and earn enough to pay for my flying lessons. But the environment—and especially the night work—was so alien to me that I had to get out in two weeks. I couldn't stand it.

My brother Lawrence and some of his mates were living at Bondi then, and my next idea was to get a taxi driver's licence, and to move over that way. In my old Holden FC, and with directory in hand, I drove the streets of the city and its suburbs, familiarising myself with the main roads, the suburbs, the hospitals. Eventually I went to a driving school and did a cab-driving course. I got my licence and for three months I drove for Yellow Cabs at Darlinghurst on the 3.00 p.m. to 1.00 a.m. shift. Once again, it wasn't really me. It was a new challenge, something different—but it wasn't what I was looking for.

So I went back to what I knew—to horses. Randwick trainer Albert McKenna, a decent bloke, gave me a job in his stables, and I worked there for six months. He put me in charge of some stables he had in Church Lane. I lived down there and had to look after the horses that were there, and get them ready for morning trackwork.

One morning Albert said to me: 'Brian, I've got a couple of horses coming in today that I want you to take care of.'

'Are they racehorses?' I asked.

'No,' he answered. 'There's a bloke who rides regularly in Centennial Park—and they're his.' I wasn't too happy about it . . .

The 'bloke' turned out to be Harry M. Miller, the entrepreneur. I can remember him pulling up out the front in a Rolls Royce, complete with chauffeur. He had all the gear on—the boots, the jodhpurs, the coat.

After a couple of days I'd had enough, and I fronted McKenna. 'Look, this is not my go,' I said. 'I'm not going to be a bloody lapdog for some rich person. I'm here for racehorses. If you want me involved in this other thing, then I'm out.'

We had a decent argument, and I had the final word—'Stick the job up your arse!' I said, and departed. It wasn't about Harry M. Miller. He might be an okay guy when you get to know him, which I didn't. It was about a principle. There was no way I was going to be a flunkey for anyone like that. The truth was, I was getting a bit restless in Sydney anyway . . .

* * *

So, I moved on, beginning a pilgrimage that I guess most people would consider pretty extraordinary. I had this idea in my head that I would get a job in a jumping stable in Melbourne, because I liked the jumpers back then. I'd watched the great 'chaser Crisp win the Cup Day Steeple at Flemington in 1969, and I thought it was an awe-inspiring sight. When I arrived at the bus station in Melbourne, I rang the only contact I had, a bloke at the McCormick jump stables. The answer was not what I'd hoped for: there were no jobs going. I sat and thought it over. I've got nowhere to stay here in Melbourne, I concluded. Bugger it, I'll keep going. So I went straight to the counter and extended my ticket to Alice Springs, and was on the next bus out of town heading that way—a long haul via Adelaide and Coober Pedy to The Alice.

My first port of call in Alice Springs was a downtown pub, where I ordered a beer. I had barely got it in my hand before a couple of blokes were alongside, pestering me for money. I looked around me. Nothing's changed, I thought. In my time as a ringer I had been used to blokes hanging around the pubs, trying to bite you for a few bob. It was then that the idea—which must have been at the back of my head for quite a while—hit me: Stuff it! I'll go back home and give training a go.

So, I got my Redline ticket extended again and took the next bus to Mt Isa. By this time I had been on the road for a week, grabbing what sleep I could on the bus, and the occasional shower and a feed when we pulled in somewhere. By Mt Isa I had had more than enough of the bus; I still had a little bit of money left, so I booked a seat on a light plane to Cairns. I finally got home with just the clothes I stood up in, a travelling bag, and ten dollars in my pocket.

* * *

Back home, I broke the news to my mum and dad: 'I'm going to give training a go—and I'm going to start here in Cairns. But I'm not going to bludge on you. I'm going to get a job and pay you board.' They seemed glad to have me back.

I did get a job, doing something I had never done before—driving trucks on the Tablelands for a road construction company, the Mohommed Brothers of Edmonton, whose business was the tip trucks used on road construction projects. The work got me a bit of a bank, but was counterproductive to an extent. I was trying to get a name in Cairns so I could get some horses to train, but the reality was that I was stuck up on the Tablelands all week, and only getting home at weekends.

With Alf Eales' help I picked up a job in town, loading hand-cut sugar cane. That was about at the tail end of the hand-cut era, and it was bloody hard work, and hot work. You were out there in the full sun, with no shade, trying to keep up with the truck as you loaded. And you had to carry this sort of big key, a ratchet, to tighten the steel chain securing the cane onto the back of the truck. That was hard going, too—you had to throw nearly your full weight against it to get the chain tight enough.

Anyhow, it was a job, and in between times, Alf, who was a keen racing man, was introducing me around among the racing community. Some of the other trainers were having a laugh at my expense—the young hotshot with the Sydney experience. As a bloke with a fairly short fuse in those days, some of it was pretty hard for me to cop. But I wore it, and waited for my chance to come. Alf Eales was the bloke who really got me started in training, along with my mother, who got me my first two horses to train, through old friends. Alf battled hard for months—and took some ridiculing along the way—as he worked at convincing owners to give me horses. I owe him a lot.

Eventually the chances came, through the support of some family friends. Kevin Schmidt, who owned the Stratford Hotel with his wife June, said to me one day: 'I'll get you a horse. I'll get one up from Brisbane.' Oh yeah, I thought. That's just talk. Then the Lucey family, butchers and cattle station owners from Gordonvale and friends of my mother's, sent a horse to me, Global Bid. In the meantime I dug into the money I had earned, and bought a horse (by Nuclear Grey) from Alan Atkinson, a member of a very well-known local family, from the Valley of Lagoons Station.

I broke him in myself, and called him Grey Pilot. But just when he was showing some potential, evidenced in a nice first run, fate dealt the sort of blow which seems to go with the territory when you get into the horseracing business. During a bad tropical storm one night, Grey Pilot broke out of the stables on Cannon Park Racecourse and galloped south down the Bruce Highway. There, adjacent to the Cairns Drive-In and not far from the track, he was struck by a truck and one of his legs was injured so badly that the vet had no choice but to put him down. By chance I wasn't at the racecourse that night—I had gone to visit my mum and dad in Stratford. It was a devastating blow, and freakish bad luck the way it happened. The stables I had for my horses were old and unlit. The gate on the yard holding

Grey Pilot was secured by a long bolt that fitted well, and held the gate firm. But the storm must have frightened him so much that he crashed into the gate, bent the bolt, and sprung the gate open.

It was a bad blow after the success I'd had with my first horse, Gay Meld, the filly that Kev Schmidt had sent up from Brisbane. I told you earlier a little about Gay Meld, how she nearly drowned me in the Mulgrave River one afternoon. But I remember her for a lot more than that. She and Global Bid laid down the foundation for me for all that followed. Gay Meld, owned by June Schmidt and her sister, Mrs Von Dobbin, won nine races, including the Gordon-vale Cup, earning both the horse and me some good publicity. Global Bid also won nine races, among them the Mareeba Cup of 1971.

I experienced the sting of professional jealousy through the early successes I had. Leading the charge was a bloke who was one of the top trainers up there. The stories got back to me, about how they were calling me the 'genius' from Sydney who had brought up a 'good hit' with him that he had got from Jack Denham. It was sour grapes—and rubbish.

I got my licence in 1971 and Gay Meld was my first winner, bolting in by ten lengths up at Mareeba on the Tablelands in April 1971. In those days they'd have a meeting on the coast every Saturday and one up on the Tablelands, usually at Mareeba or Atherton. Mareeba was no glamour circuit but it was functional, with all you needed for a race meeting: rails, a grandstand, an enclosure, a secretary's office, jockeys' room, stables, and prize money.

I remember the day very well. The filly had not long since arrived from Brisbane and I honestly didn't know much about her. At training, though, and around the stables she had been very good, pretty much trouble-free. On the float to Mareeba that first day, she was a bit nervy, and was still that way when I led her into the ring. When I went to leg up the jockey, Maxie King, she just reared straight up in the air. And she did it every time he got near her, landing with a front leg over the enclosure fence at one point. Eventually Maxie had to swing on as I was trotting her along the track. She was okay from that point, and won handsomely, by ten lengths. There were only three runners!

She was my first starter in a race and that night I celebrated with Kevin and June Schmidt, really nice people who owned the pub in Mareeba as well as the one at Stratford. Prize money was $250, from memory. No fortune. But at least I was on my way, and the Schmidts were delighted. Owning a successful racehorse is great fare for a publican—a talking point around the bar, a shared interest with patrons, an interesting extra dimension to the publicans' life (outside throwing kegs around and pulling beers).

Among her various successes, Gay Meld won the Gordonvale Cup, the big event at the main Gordonvale meeting of the year. It was quite a finish and, at 4/1, she pipped the favourite, Royal Robber, in controversial circumstances. It was the first time they had used the photo finish apparatus up there, and after they went across the line the judge put the numbers up the other way around. He thought the favourite, on the inside, had won the race. But when the print came down, mine had won by a lip. How fortunate that was, that the photo finish camera had arrived in Gordonvale for that meeting. There was great excitement at the gate takings on a record day at Gordonvale—$1070.

The photo finish camera unveiled at Gordonvale was state of the art in that neck of the woods back then—and how. I remember well the more unorthodox method used by the judge at the Mingela course, Mingela being a halfway point between Townsville and Charters Towers, up on the

Great Dividing Range. They only raced a couple of times a year there, and it was one of those real bush meetings. The judge at Mingela came up with the ingenious idea of punching a couple of eyeholes in an empty Fourex carton, then putting it over his head to adjudicate on races. His theory was that with the box over his head, nothing else would distract his line of vision. So, that's how the races were judged—by a bloke with a beer box over his head. Getting rid of the contents of the carton in the first place would have been no major problem either, that being a thirsty part of the world.

It was cattle country, grazing country, and I had spent a little time around there when I was at school at Mt Carmel. Near to Mingela there was an army camp, at a place called Selheim, and the school cadets would go there once a year on bivouac, staying in the barracks and training in the surrounding bushland. I remember it mainly for the fact that it was there, early one morning, that I heard of the death of Marilyn Monroe, via a tiny transistor radio while we were having breakfast. I remember being shocked, and pretty sad about it for the rest of the day.

⁂

As well as Gay Meld, the Schmidt family also leased a horse called Quran, which had won a few races under the leading trainer in Cairns, Max Hanson, and then hit the wall. When I first went down to have a look at her in the paddock at Babinda, she was badly cut around the legs, the result of a collision with the fence, and she had proud flesh around the wounds. She had just been thrown into the paddock and left there, and was as skinny as a rake, the grass up there not being of much use to racehorses as feed. Anyhow, I nursed her back and got her good and healthy, and she raced her way from a low division all the way up to top division. She ended up winning seven or eight races and Kevin Schmidt always got a kick out of ribbing Tom Judas, the bloke who had leased the horse to him: 'Have you got any more that you can lease to us?' he would ask with a grin.

In the early days I won a double at the Cairns Amateurs with Quran and an old horse that had originally come up from Sydney, Grenoble Boy. Dick Chant, the course broadcaster and ABC commentator, gave me a bit of a wrap on FNQ television news that night: 'There's a young man who trained a double today—and you're going to hear a lot more of him,' he said.

As a rookie trainer I had pretty simple but firm ideas. I just felt that if you fed the horses well and worked them hard without hammering them, the fitness would develop. And if you placed them right, and if the horse had ability and you had the right jockey, then the horse would do the rest. And that's pretty well the way it's been for me, from back then to now. I am very lucky to have done as well as I have because, in truth, I never really had a good education in the horse-training business. Throughout my career, I have just stuck to the simple things. From my early contacts like Mazzaglia and Denham, I learned only the basics. I was self-taught, really, and because I don't come from a racing background, there was never anything really to fall back on in the way of special knowledge. The thing that made it happen for me was basically my persistence and the goal I set myself. I was so totally focused and committed to that, I wouldn't allow anything to sway me from it. It is, I'm sure, what got me there in the end . . .

CHAPTER SEVEN

Setting the Bar High

My goal. This story is exactly as it happened, one afternoon at Cannon Park Racecourse, Cairns, very early in my new career as a horse trainer, when I sat and yarned with an old bloke named Wally Holmes. Wally was a terrific old guy; he loved racing, and he loved having a punt. His son-in-law was a local bookie, which fuelled his interest even further. He used to come out and keep me company, maybe have a beer when I'd finished work at the end of the day. I was living on the course in a caravan—I'll tell you more about that later—and I'm sure Wally felt sorry for me. He probably thought, this poor bugger is stuck out here on his own; he must be going mad. All he does is look after the horses.

I liked Wally a lot. Retired by then, he'd been a very successful businessman in town, one of the head honchos at Burns Philp, but a bloke with the common touch. Anyway, we were sitting in the caravan late one afternoon, on about our second beer, and I said to him, 'You know, one day I'm going to be the leading trainer in Sydney.'

There was a pregnant pause while Wally took it in and then he just said this: 'Well, Brian, that is very admirable. I hope in time you won't be disappointed.' It was probably his nice way of saying that I was shooting for the sky and that what I was aiming for was a bit rich. But he didn't reject it. And for my own part, I held the thought firmly in my mind always, even through the doubting times, and kept pushing myself towards what must have seemed an impossible dream.

In those days I lived in a small second-hand caravan parked under a big old Moreton Bay fig tree at Cannon Park Racecourse. When it rained or blew, the figs would plop onto the roof of my caravan. I didn't have two cents to rub together, but I was determined to do it myself and not bludge off my parents. They offered help, but I said, 'I'm on my own now—you've helped me enough.' I lived that way for two years.

As time went on, I only ever had a maximum of six to eight horses, and I looked after them all myself. I never employed anyone. Blokes used to tell me how they'd be having a cold beer of an afternoon in the Woree Hotel nearby and they'd look across and see me walking horses in the car park in the heat. 'Have a look at that poor bastard,' they'd say to each other. 'He's got to go off his head . . . he can't keep that up.' Sometimes I would skip meals and at times I felt as though my body was weakening because I didn't have enough food to sustain me for the work I was doing seven days a week. But I got through.

Initially I rode all my own trackwork. The stables were not much more than sheds in those early days, with no lights. I'd get up at three-thirty to do the boxes in the dark via the light from one of those kerosene hurricane lamps. This was a bit unnerving owing to the fact that there was a large carpet snake living along the rafters, which weren't very high at all. I was always aware of his presence. Around country track stables you'll generally get a snake or two, but even though I've been in the bush for a fair bit of my life, snakes still put the breeze up me.

⁂

The fact is that my career as a trainer was almost over a year or so after it began. When I started out in Cairns, I struck the wettest wet season they'd had for many years. It poured—torrential rain day after day, virtually from January through to May, making life even more difficult and probably adding an edge to my already hot temper.

One Saturday afternoon about twelve months after I'd become a trainer, I had a horse called Torrential racing in the last at Cairns. After the race I had him in the hosing bay, which is right next to the car park at Cannon Park, when my brother Lawrence and a couple of his mates came over and Lawrence said to me, 'There are a few blokes and a sheila over there giving the old man and Mum a hard time.' He told me they'd tried to pull a seat out from under my father when he went to sit down. Immediately I switched to aggressive mode. 'Where are they?' I asked.

There were people streaming out of the course after the last, and Lawrence pointed: 'That's them there,' he said. There were three blokes and a girl, so I headed over to them and said, 'So who's the smartarse who takes on old people?' They looked at each other: 'Who's he talking to? Who are you?'

'Is this the bloke?' I asked Lawrence. 'Yeah, I'm pretty sure it is,' he answered. Lawrence's mate Harry, standing alongside, nodded. So, I just whacked the bloke, and down he went. Then the second bloke had a go, and I got into him. Meanwhile Lawrence was getting stuck into the third of the trio. When I had the second bloke down, someone jumped on my back and put their hands over my eyes. In the heat of battle I brought my elbow around and landed one fair in the ribs. There was a grunt and my attacker fell away. It turned out to be the girlfriend of the bloke I had down, which was a worry for me because I never, ever hit females. She had chosen to join in, which wasn't that lady-like, and the result had been predictable.

It was a huge commotion, with people milling around everywhere, and through the noise I heard the announcement: 'Would the police please go immediately to the car park!' At that point Paddy Ryan, who had been a top jockey up that way and was now a trainer and a pal, grabbed me. 'Mate, get out of here,' he said. 'If they catch you, you'll lose your licence.' I was still hot and ready to go on with it, but Lawrence said, 'Yeah, c'mon . . . get going.'

On the Monday, Tom Carlton, Chief Steward of the Cairns Racing Club, called me into the office. 'Brian, I've heard about that problem on Saturday,' he said. 'You can't do that sort of thing; you're a licensed person.'

'I know that, Tom, but this is a different case,' I said. 'This involved my family, and I'll be straightforward with you, whatever you do with me—I'll tell you I would have to do the same thing again if the circumstances were the same. I don't go looking for trouble, but I don't walk away from it either.'

Carlton looked at me. 'I'm going to have to refer this to Townsville,' he said. 'We'll have to wait and see.' In a couple of days, he conveyed the result: 'Brian, you're right this time, but *please* don't do it again.'

You wouldn't want to know, but three or four months later a bloke picked me in the bar at Innisfail races. I had a bit of rum in me—I used to drink rum in those days—and it would fire me up. To cut a long story short, I decked him.

'Brian, what have you *done*?' said Tom Carlton when the news got back to Cairns. 'You just can't keep doing this!' Somehow, through the generosity and understanding of Carlton, I got off again that time. The fact is that it could all have finished right there. I could have been struck off as a licensed person, and that probably would have been the end of me as a horse trainer.

* * *

When I was asked to tell my story in this book, and I thought about doing that, I knew the one thing I had to be was honest. I don't want people saying: 'Look at this bloke—what a great guy. Never done anything wrong.' Because that is not the truth of it. My story is not a rosy one.

The fact is that one of the biggest handicaps I have had to deal with in my life is a bad temper, bordering on explosive. The stories in this chapter from my early days as a trainer in Cairns are a reflection of that reality. In earlier days this temper was almost like a bloody demon which came riding out of the dark recesses of my mind and trampled everyone in its path. I have been brutal to people at times, and caused lasting damage. I have hurt with words—and once something is said, it can't be unsaid.

Along the journey of my life I have bruised people, put myself offside with people, made myself unapproachable. It is a difficulty that I have had to handle. It is not something that I desired, or enjoyed doing—probably it has been a sort of weakness within. Maybe in some ways the demon that was my travelling companion also knocked down some doors for me, eliminated some of the opposition. But sometimes it has been tough baggage to carry. As I write this book, the reality is that I am offside with my two brothers Lawrence and Noel, and my sister is the only family member I talk to.

There are two sides to every story, but the truth is that I am far from blameless in the situations that developed with my brothers. With them, the fabric is torn pretty badly. But I should say that both my brothers in their own different ways have helped me in my career and, no matter what, I never forget.

I am a calmer person since Maree, my wife since 1985, came into my life . . . and since Africa. Maree sums me up when she says: 'Brian blows up quick, but it can be forgotten moments later. Once he's got it out of his system, he's fine. But the problem can be with the other person, who may never forget.' Fortunately, as I got older, I learned there was a better way of doing things.

✖✖✖

I digress. The way I was back then got me into serious trouble in Cairns when I first started training all those years ago—and probably I was lucky to survive. When I eventually got to Sydney years later, Tom Carlton was on the stewards' panel there and we used to have a chuckle about the days 'back home'.

My ambition and the long-term goal I had shared with Wally Holmes in Cairns took me south to Townsville in late 1972. The second stepping stone. I was going well in Cairns then, and when it was apparent I was thinking of leaving, the raceclub secretary, John O'Brien, came to me with an offer: 'Don't go to Townsville,' he said. 'We've got a syndicate of people who will buy a group of horses. We'll charge them and pay you, so you won't have to worry any more about cash flow and all that.'

It was a tempting offer to someone still pretty much living off the smell of an oily rag, but in Townsville the prize money was better. For an ambitious young bloke it was the logical next step up the ladder. 'I've got to keep moving. It's time to go,' I said to John O'Brien.

'What happens if you go to Townsville and it doesn't work out?' he asked.

'It's a chance I've got to take,' I said. I knew what I was doing—and I knew what I wanted. In the interest of backing my belief, I refused an offer that other local trainers would probably have killed for.

I moved south in 1974, without much style. I threw my gear into the back of Alf Eales' four-wheel drive and Mum drove my second-hand Holden wagon, with the Globetrotter caravan hooked on the back, and in procession we made the trek to Cluden Racecourse, Townsville. I parked the van at a spot up near the turn into the straight under a shady tree, and that became my home.

Good fortune smiled on me. As I had done in Cairns (and was to do further south), I won with my first starter in Townsville, a horse called Don't Delay who whipped the smart Brisbane sprinter Travelling Man by five lengths. I followed up with another win soon afterwards, through Pampelone. With the money I got out of the early winners I was able to upgrade the caravan to a roomier model. Money was certainly in short supply in those early days as a trainer. I worked from daylight to dark, lived in a caravan, and lived as cheaply as I could. I carted my horses around in an old two-horse trailer. Memory tells me that in Cairns I charged my owners $20 a week. And I was considered expensive!

Don't Delay, who kick-started me in Townsville, had shown considerable promise in Cairns, where he won a few races. He was pretty much the reason I went to Townsville, winning the final race at the Cairns meeting of 29 June 1972, and so being my last runner at the track where it had all begun. I thought, here's a horse good enough to make an impression for me, good enough to give me the chance of hitting Townsville with a bang. Another mare I took down, Pampelone, won her first two starts very impressively. So I hit the ground running.

Townsville was to be a relatively happy time for me. I stayed for about two years and had pretty good success even without winning any of the big cups. An old trainer there, Clete Davies, was very good to me. He helped smooth the path for me in that town, sharing with me his own beliefs about racing and training.

My thoughts on training horses probably haven't changed too much from what they were in those formative years in Cairns and Townsville. I think that to give yourself a chance of success you've got to have a bit of an 'eye' for a horse, and I've probably always had that, having been around horses so long. A lot of it is down to commonsense. I remember that when I first went to Cairns, the local trainers said to me: 'You can't keep horses here, or feed them the way you do in the south. It's too hot—they'll heat up too much.'

I thought about that and I knew that if I was training a boxer up there in Cairns, I'd feed him exactly the same as I would if he was in Sydney. So I just went ahead and did what I wanted to do, which was basically look after my horses well, feed them well and train them hard so their fitness would carry them through. That philosophy has never changed. I did, as well, keep the electrolytes up to them—something I never let on to anybody about.

Chapter Eight

Heading South

When I started off in racing, I used to punt—and I did all right early. Beginner's luck, no doubt! Because the truth of it was that I didn't know too much. After a time I figured it out for myself: you know you can't win at this; you might get in front for a while, but they will beat you in the end. So I gave it away.

It started way back for me, in the late fifties when I went to Cairns races one day with some people from across the street, the Skarrotts. I was mates with one of their boys. I backed a horse called Gallant Lad, picking him because the name appealed, and he duly won the race. How good is this? I thought.

The fact is, I've always been a bit tight-fisted—although I've always been happy to help people who genuinely needed help. Even on that first day at the races, I pocketed my winnings, didn't have another bet and took the money home to put in the piggy bank. I can recall as a kid both

Lawrence and me being given ten bob each by our parents when we went to the Cairns Show, back in the days when the rides were sixpence a go. Lawrence would have blown his in half an hour and be back for more. I'd eke mine out and finish up spending about half, keeping the other five bob to take home to put in the money box.

The second time I went to the races was when I was back in Cairns on holidays. On that particular day I had a series of bets in three states—six bets in all, and came up with five winners! By the time I lined up to collect the last couple, the bloke at the bookie's stand was saying: 'Shit—not you again!' But the success on the punt whetted my appetite only a little. Back at work in the bush I wasn't much interested; if the races came on the radio, I would switch over to a music station. I dabbled only now and then after that. In Brisbane, Tony Erhart and I used to have a bit of a system going when I was at the Mazzaglia stable, but I was never too hooked on the punting business.

In my life I have always had a firm inclination that once I get hold of something, I am not going to give it up. And that's why punting for me is essentially a waste of time, and money. I enjoy the horses themselves, but for me there is not much enjoyment in winning a few dollars. I know from experience, too, that you can turn into a bit of a desperado when you become a punter–trainer, and that your judgment can be affected in relation to particular horses which might 'owe' you money.

A small trainer who punts is more likely to back his horse up quickly after a losing run, chasing his money. Probably the horse is not ready, needs a bit more time—and gets beaten again. And so the cycle continues, with emotion overpowering commonsense. I recall clearly the words of Fil Allota when I moved to Sydney and he let me use his stables at Randwick. He was a great trainer as far as I was concerned. He only ever had a small team, but he always came up with top horses. I remember the first time he said to me, 'Even though I bet myself, the truth is that punter–trainers generally end up with a sandshoe and a galosher.' It stuck in my mind, underpinning my own philosophy. Some people just love a bet. For me, it is of no interest.

Progressively over the years my preference was, and is, for non-punting owners too. It makes life less complicated. I have always been a percentage man; my livelihood as a trainer is from the percentage I can win, not from anything to do with gambling. I have long realised that most of the time in your life you don't make spectacular gains. What counts is persistence—if you can keep doggedly pushing on, you'll eventually get over the top of what you are aiming for.

It can take time. Until I joined up with Mrs Millie Fox in Sydney and got the benefit of being a private trainer of a large team of horses, I was virtually on the bones of my arse. From the time I started in Cairns until Maree came along and *made* me take a holiday—a week on South Molle Island—I didn't miss one day's work in eleven years, except for the time that my fracas with Gay Meld in the river at Gordonvale put me in hospital. Even in my hospital bed I was working mentally, probably wound up more than ever before, in fact, worrying about my horses and feeling absolutely helpless because I was flat on my back.

The work was unrelenting, but it was what I had chosen to do, and I make no complaint. Training horses through those early years meant working 365 days a year, every year. Sunday brought a lighter load at least, although there was still feeding and walking to be done. Until I came to Sydney, bringing with me the apprentice Rodney Hardwick, I did virtually everything myself. In Brisbane I'd had a couple of employees, plus the support of my brother Lawrence.

In quieter times over the years I have often questioned what I do in my working life. I suppose we all do that now and then. My motivation has changed in more recent times. I do what I do these days so I can be of some small, tangible help to the endangered animals of Africa. But in the mid-1980s, when I was flying high at Nebo Lodge, my answers to this question were:

- I was fulfilling an ambition.
- I loved horses above all else.
- By doing it, I had created a comfortable existence.

In the life of a racehorse trainer, just about every day is a 4.00 a.m. start. In Melbourne these days I work every second Sunday—a 6.00 a.m. start to about 9.30 a.m., then back for an hour and a half in the afternoon to feed up and do the boxes. In between times there are numerous telephone calls, nominations to be worked out, arrangements for horses to be moved, getting to race meetings, trying to fit in the normal things of life . . . and plenty more. And it doesn't let up.

Over the years, and from my early days in Cairns and Townsville, I got into the routine of preparing all trackwork the previous night. I like it to be all set up so that everyone at the stables knows exactly what is going on. I like things to run like clockwork. The plan is: get things done, get them done properly, and get finished. The big problem for me can come at the other end of the day if I happen to go out to dinner with any of the owners. By about nine or nine-thirty, it's all catching up with me and I'm falling asleep. Sometimes I reckon they must be thinking, he's a boring bastard, this bloke. Most of them understand, I'm sure, but I never feel too good about it. After all, they've taken some trouble, they want to have a yarn and be in your company—and you're there bloody going to sleep on them!

I still find the early mornings tough after all these years—

the 3.30 a.m. alarm. And especially so on a mid-winter morning in Melbourne when you can hear the wind and rain lashing outside, and you think, Oh, no. But we're all the same. Once you're up and around for five minutes, you're okay. I suppose most people would view it as a punishing schedule, but I decided pretty early in life that there were no free rides. And if you want something that no-one else has, then you have to really make sacrifices.

⁂

Three things led me on from Townsville to the next stage of my inevitable progress south: a good horse, an owner who trusted me, and the goal I had set myself—to climb to the top of the tree in Sydney. In Townsville I struck up a friendship with a guy named Gil Jacques, who trained horses. Gil was pretty suspicious of people, which is not a bad way to be when you're in the racing game, but he liked me and thought that I was genuine.

He had a terrific sprinter named Torbadol, and when he couldn't take the horse to Brisbane, having decided that Torbadol was certainly good enough to have a crack at city class—and I had made up my mind that I was heading down there—he gave me the horse to train. Gil wanted to use the Townsville-based jockeys Paul Gordy and Billy Bethel, top jocks in the north, on the horse's campaign. Gordy in fact won on him at Torbadol's first start at Doomben, bringing him down the outside in a Clayfield Transition (1200 m) for his ninth win in a row, but when Billy Bethel rode him next start, it didn't work out, the horse finishing fourth. I said to Gil: 'I've got nothing against Paul or Bill. They're good jockeys, but they're Townsville jockeys. If you want to give this horse every chance down here, you've got to put on the best available.' Gil took my advice. After Torbadol got beaten in his second start in town, I put Mick Dittman on, and, I think, Tony Erhart rode him once. He won his next five straight.

Torbadol was my first starter in a race in Brisbane. I had maintained my record of winning 'first up' in a new town. He came south not long after the evening I had loaded my other four horses (The Busker, Bobby Dazzler, Don't Delay and Bold Gauntlet) onto a truck hired from Brisbane Livestock in Townsville in early 1974 and headed to Brisbane. The nicely bred Red Rumour horse The Busker won at the Gold Coast and placed in town, but the other three were injured, or went wrong—a trend that plagued me in those early, teething days in Brisbane.

Torbadol was the star—a very, very good horse. He was something of a rarity, in fact. There weren't too many horses up to that time that had come down from North Queensland to make the sort of impact that he did in the city. It happens more these days when there's racing every day, and the horses are spread so thin. Back then there were metropolitan meetings on Saturday and Wednesday, a provincial meeting Thursday, and that was it. The fields were big and the races tough to win. And when there were handy horses around you couldn't dodge them, because there weren't that many races available.

Chapter Nine

The 'Big Smoke'

The shift to Brisbane, when it came in 1974, was nothing glamorous. For most of the time there I lived out on the Nudgee Road, in a single room under a typical 'Queenslander' set high on its wooden stumps and owned by an old lady named Betty Saunders. It was no palace, I can tell you. My room had just one window, of glass louvres, and to get to the outside world, I had to walk through the laundry, dodging the washing. Out front the big trucks rolled endlessly down Nudgee Road, rattling the house to its foundations.

At least I was back in a house. I sold the caravan before I left Townsville, and my car too, and was sitting up front with the truck driver, the horses behind, when I left town to try my luck in the 'big smoke'. We headed for Deagon, out near Sandgate, and I set up my base there for about six months. Then I managed to get some stables at Hendra, closer in. I trained my horses at Doomben.

I set out my goals to the *Courier Mail*'s Allen Voltz: 'I don't want to be a big "plunge" man, winning few races and getting money in bundles. I'm after a good average and a nice percentage.'

At least I had some help in Brisbane. Lawrence had become interested in racing when I got involved, and had eventually taken the step himself. After a spell with the Department of Main Roads in downtown Sydney, he had worked at both the Pat Murray and Bart Cummings stables. When I shifted south, he moved north, from Sydney, and basically the two of us ran the whole operation. I felt I was learning all the time, and Brisbane was another chapter in my racing education. As I mentioned earlier, my brother and I don't get on these days, but his coming to Brisbane helped me build a good solid platform to work off. Perhaps I could have done it on my own, but it certainly made it easier, him being there.

Sydney, though, continued to burn brightly in my own mind. I still didn't really have a clue how it was going to happen, but I consoled myself with the thought that I was making progress, getting closer. All of a sudden, in a reasonably short space of time, I had taken the step of coming from being a nobody in Cairns to becoming a trainer in Brisbane, earning some respect and doing quite well.

I have always been a realistic person, but I think you've always got to do your best to be positive too. It's hard for all of us to fight the negatives that creep into our minds, but I have always believed in the importance of facing things as positively as you can. In those early years when I was getting a toehold in racing, my policy, essentially, was just to keep going, to press on. I worked hard, was persistent—and I know a hell of a lot of people share those qualities. Even now when I think back on it, the way things fell into place in my life in racing still amazes me. It seemed that whenever

I needed a break, a break came. It was so far from where I'd come from to end up where I did—so much luck was needed for that. After all, I had so little ability and so little experience in comparison with so many others who had been in the game for years and years. It almost seemed like I was destined by some greater force to get the breaks I needed—that fate was steering my ship.

One thing I have learned in life is that there are many people who work *very* hard and never get anywhere much. Somehow, they just don't seem to get the breaks, and unless you *do* get some breaks in your life, then you probably won't make it. But at the same time, I reckon you have to position yourself so that you *can* get the breaks—set the bar high, give yourself something to shoot for. So many people work like donkeys, thinking of nothing else but the next task, thinking no further than that, not thinking of anything grander. At the same time, I do believe in the saying, 'The harder you work, the luckier you get'.

Oh, yes, I got some breaks all right. Even back at the beginning in Cairns, when people didn't know me. The thing was, they knew my mother, so they gave me horses to train because of their regard for her. And Gil Jacques in Townsville, with Torbadol—he could so easily have said, 'No, I'm going to take him to Brisbane myself.' But he didn't—he gave the horse to me. And because of Torbadol, who won seven city races, I got off the ground there. The other horses I took wouldn't have done that for me.

I only ever had a small team in Brisbane, but I won fourteen races in the first twelve months, so it was a solid start. One I remember was a horse called Prefecture, who actually won Race No 14 for me in the first year. He was a wind-sucker, and his neck was deeply scarred where they'd operated on him to try and solve the problem. It didn't work. It's a strange thing that happens with some horses—

out of boredom, they'll grab onto the edge of the door, or the box in the stable, and suck in air to the extent that it can upset their whole digestive system.

But if I had breaks—and I did—I had my share of bad fortune too. For a time in my training career I was plagued by a run of sick or broken-down horses. The list was a long one: Don't Delay, Cool Sunset, The Busker, Bold Gauntlet (which cut a leg while swimming), Bobby Dazzler (which had a large fetlock which was always going to come against him one day), and even Torbadol, the star of the stable. All of them were struck down with different things. It wasn't as if there was some sort of unique problem in the stables. Torbadol, for example, contracted travel sickness while being transported back to Townsville, and it really knocked him around. I had to turn him out for a long spell, and he was never the same horse after it. The succession of problems was no greater than the way it can be, and is, in the racing game. It is a business of peaks and troughs, and the trick is to relax in the lean times, keep your head down and keep going, knowing that, for sure, something better lies ahead.

For me, having wrestled with the string of problems that befell my horses in Brisbane, the upswing began with a horse named Tiger Town. He was a big, powerful colt, bought by Roley Norris and Kev Davies for $9500 at the Sydney yearling sales. Henry Davis, an established Brisbane trainer, usually looked after Roley Norris's horses and in fact had trained Tiger Town's half-brother, Lion City, who was very handy. But Tiger Town was a big, heavy horse who, as a two year old, had already developed splints and had been pinfired. Roley's belief was that the Henry Davis method—Henry trained his horses very hard on the way to getting them fit—would not suit Tiger Town, so he picked me out. He didn't know me but he picked me anyway, maybe because of the work I had done with 'difficult' horses in recent times. I trained the horse with a fairly delicate hand. I was mindful of his leg problems and took it quietly, swimming him a lot, keeping a close eye on him. But despite the doubts about his legs, he coped with it all very well. I don't ever remember him struggling that much. He was a quiet, strong horse. He just always seemed that way.

He was also one of those horses who managed to capture the imagination of the public to an extent and who, as a result, attracted a good deal of publicity. Inevitably when that happens, the trainer gets carried along with it. Horses like Torbadol and Tiger Town helped put my name upfront, helped get me some respect, ability-wise and character-wise. Tiger Town raced his way through the ranks in Brisbane and by 1976 was obviously bound for bigger things. He was the best horse I had had to that point, although Torbadol wasn't that far behind him.

As it turned out, he was also my ticket to Sydney, and the big time . . .

CHAPTER TEN

'They Tried to Steal My Horse'

I'll never forget how Sydney racing's big guns, Tommy Smith and Perc Galea, tried to undermine me when I brought Tiger Town south in 1976. The big horse was a stranger to the Randwick track on his first run in town, a 1600-metres welter, and started hanging out from the 1000-metre mark. He just kept drifting wide from that point, despite the efforts of jockey Gary Palmer, rounding the turn seven or eight wide, and finishing up almost on the outside fence. But he won. Brilliantly. And landed a $100,000 betting plunge in the process. That made it ten wins from seventeen starts. Behind him in the placings that day were a couple of pretty fair horses in Tuscany and Rose of Kingston. In Sydney we housed him at the Randwick stables of Jack Mandel, then eighty-six, the man who had bred Tiger Town.

Smith and Galea tried to pinch Tiger Town off me almost before I had pulled the saddle off him that day. They descended on the owners while I was talking to the jockey immediately after the race! Smith took Roley Norris out to dinner that night and, as I found out later, did his utmost to convince him of the wisdom of the horse being switched to his stable. Roley told me later that Smith had offered to train the horse for half the (fairly modest) fee I was charging. 'I just wanted to go out to dinner with him to see how he operated,' said Norris of Smith, explaining later what had taken place. Later, there were reports of an offer from Bart Cummings asking Tiger Town's owners to put a price on the horse. They declined.

My realisation about Smith's move did not endear him to me in any way. And none of the sparse dealings I had with him in the years that followed made me change my view of the bloke. The memory of what he and Perc Galea tried to do in relation to Tiger Town (it wasn't as though Tommy was short of horses!) provided me with vast satisfaction on a memorable day some years down the track. You might have gathered by now that I don't go looking for trouble, although in earlier years it found *me* often enough. But I am a square-up merchant. If someone does me a wrong, well, I just keep it in mind—and if the opportunity ever comes along, I'll square up. And so it turned out between me and the famous T.J. Smith. Sometimes, what goes around, comes around . . .

To the credit of both owners, Roley Norris and Kev Davies, and to my everlasting good fortune, they stuck solid, putting stock on old values and leaving Tiger Town in my care. But their decision to leave the horse with me carried with it conditions. 'Look, Brian,' said Norris, 'this is the way it is: if you want to hang on to Tiger Town, you will have to move to Sydney. If you feel you can't do that, I will give him to another trainer at Randwick.'

The cards were on the table—a fair request, I reckoned—

and from my point of view it didn't require much thought. I had been in Brisbane for two years by then and a new door of opportunity had opened. My early-days dream of a Sydney premiership was as strong as ever in my mind. This now was the chance to at least get a toe in the water of Sydney racing.

So I said yes, and came to Sydney to try to find the Randwick stable accommodation that had to be part of the deal. I went to the AJC and they told me there was none available. 'You might try Fil Allota,' the AJC's Billy Cooper added, almost as an afterthought. 'Though I doubt you'll do any good. Neville Begg [another Sydney trainer] tried to get some horses in at Fil's place recently, but Fil didn't want them there.' Allota was a Sydney trainer of the old school, a man who had had great horses: Cabochon, Betelgeuse, Baguette. But he had had health problems, suffering a stroke eighteen months earlier which had really knocked him around.

On a blazing hot, late spring afternoon in November 1976, figuring I had nothing to lose, I went around to Fil and Eileen Allota's place at Doncaster Avenue, Kensington, adjacent to the course, and knocked on the screen door at the back. I introduced myself to Fil at the door and he said, 'Yes, I know who you are,' and invited me in for a cup of tea. I told him straight why I was there; there was no point beating around the bush. 'How many other horses would you be bringing down?' he asked. 'You can't just live off one horse.' I told him I planned to bring six or seven others. He considered for a moment. 'Yes, that's okay,' he said.

Fate had intervened again. Fil didn't know me from a bar of soap, yet he knew Neville Begg very well. And Neville was a lovely man, liked and respected by his peers. Yet he had said 'no' to Neville and 'yes' to me. So, what exactly had happened there? I have often thought about that.

In his second start in Sydney, Tiger Town ran second in the weight-for-age Hill Stakes at Rosehill after missing the start by two lengths, and casting a plate in the run. The winner that day, Ngawyni, was a top horse. It was a sensational run and my hopes were high that he could win the Epsom at Randwick the following Saturday.

Tiger Town had only 47.5 kilograms in the $100,000 Epsom and I made the decision to keep the Brisbane lightweight Gary Palmer on him, despite what I felt was unwarranted criticism of Palmer in the race he'd won at Randwick. Yeah, he was still an apprentice, but he had won races on the course and he was an *outstanding* apprentice who knew Tiger Town better than anyone else capable of riding at that weight. We were a young team—the trainer was twenty-nine, and the jockey sixteen!

Well, Tiger Town got beaten by a lip, sending me—misty-eyed, angry and disappointed—to a secluded chair behind the grandstand after the race. It couldn't have been any closer. Tommy Smith had about five in the race and so did Bart Cummings, yet my bloke went to the front 1000 metres out, fought all the challengers off with tremendous courage after being headed, only to be pipped by Cummings' 100/1 bolter La Neige—the least fancied of his runners—who had come with a charmed run along the fence.

It was a bitter blow. When they hit the line, I thought he had won. The photo showed otherwise. La Neige ran second-last at her next start, last at the next—and then they retired the mare to stud. Tiger Town, so valiant in defeat that day, was a good but unlucky horse. Later, he was to run second in the Stradbroke—after not having had a race start for three months!

***

It was on the night of the 1976 Epsom, on 3 October, that I met Maree Fitzgerald—in not exactly ideal circumstances.

The way Maree tells it, I was still crying into my beer over Tiger Town's misfortune. I'd prefer to say that I was *whinge-ing* into my beer. This is how Maree remembers the night:

> My girlfriend, Anne Marshall, and I had gone to the Glen-synd Motel [adjacent to Randwick Racecourse] and Anne ended up sitting at the bar with Brian. After a while I thought, 'God, how is she putting up with that!' Brian was having this great whinge about being beaten in the Epsom, and Anne happens to be the sort of person who is never rude to anyone. She'll always sit and listen to someone who's got a problem. She really got stuck with him that night.

I'm pleased to say that things eventually picked up, although it was no whirlwind romance after that first casual meeting. We met again in 1981, around the time that Brin-disi won the Metropolitan. We hit it off pretty well, and things developed from there. Previously, Maree had been in the racing industry, working as a strapper at Bart Cum-mings' stables, and progressively we found we had much in common, including a shared love of animals. We've been pretty much together ever since. It was a longish courtship. We were married in 1985, at a church in suburban Strath-field, with the reception back at Nebo Lodge afterwards. There was no honeymoon. Racing people, in the main, don't have the luxury of holidays.

Over the years there has been a great sort of melding of two people with basically the same ideas. I am very lucky to have someone like her who shares my interests—and espe-cially so in being as passionate about the wildlife issue as I am, and who can blend in with my lifestyle. Maree is not the sort of person who wants to go out partying and throwing money around. She pitches in. It was nothing unusual at all that on a bitterly cold Sunday morning in Melbourne in late May 2000—with me temporarily on the sidelines after an operation—she was down at Flemington, working with the horses. 'If I don't go they'll be short-handed down there,' she said. How many trainers' wives would do that, I wonder?

Our house near Flemington is full of beautiful touches, images of Africa that have been retained in suburban Melbourne. I am sure if it had been left to me it would have been a pretty bloody bland-looking place. But there is a fair bit of creative talent in Maree's family, and she has certainly inherited it and built on it.

But I am jumping ahead . . .

* * *

For all the disappointment of the Epsom photo finish of 1976, I had 'arrived', to an extent, in Sydney. I spelled Tiger Town after the Epsom, at Roseneath Stud out near Cobbity, and went back to Brisbane to tidy up my affairs. By that time Lawrence had the urge to train, so he took over my stables and some of my horses and I made the permanent move to Sydney, bringing with me apprentice jockey Rodney Hardwick and a small string of horses which included Tiger Town, Blanc Visage, Phil's Image and Radana.

In December 1976, I was granted a licence to train at Randwick. With my horses, and Rodney and I sharing the workload, I began the long haul up to the 1980s and the successes that, unknowingly, awaited me there.

I lived in a strapper's room at the stables and my cheque book used to fluctuate between zero and about a thousand dollars. My main 'dining room' was the modest Winning Post cafe up the hill in Belmore Road, Randwick. During this time of struggle I had lots of sit-down yarns with Fil Allota and grew to know and respect him even more.

Then, once more in my life, one fateful moment, a development right out of the blue, made all the difference.

Chapter Eleven

The Hand of Fate

One morning in the early autumn of 1978, I was working with the horses at Fil Allota's stables when Eileen Allota called me from the back door. 'Brian, there is a Ken Ennever on the phone. He wants to have a word with you.' I knew of Ken well enough. As Mrs Millie Fox's stable manager he was an important player in the large Fox racing outfit. I wondered what he wanted with me.

After we had exchanged pleasantries, Ken Ennever got down to it: 'Brian, Mrs Fox asked me to give you a call. She'd like to talk to you. The situation is this: Jack Denham is leaving us. Mrs Fox is looking for another trainer and she is keen to have a yarn with you to see if you might be interested.'

I was taken aback. 'Yeah, I'd be interested all right,' I told him, 'but why would Mrs Fox be interested in *me*? I've got eight or nine horses and there are plenty of established trainers who have won group races and have much bigger names than me.' I asked him straight: 'What are you doing—approaching a group of trainers and then coming up with a short list?'

'No,' he said. 'You're the only one Mrs Fox has in mind. Could you make some time to come up to her home at Clareville? We can show you the horses we've got and have a yarn about the whole thing.' Of course, I said yes.

Millie Fox was the widow of Stan Fox, the coal-mining, manufacturing and engineering magnate who had bought and built up the stables in the 1960s after Mrs Fox had told him she'd 'love to own a beautiful racehorse'. The late Stan Fox, a blacksmith by trade, had made his fortune largely from coal trucks and from a foundry in the western suburbs of Sydney. Stan and Millie had set up their own racing empire at Nebo Lodge, Rosehill, with Jack Denham as their trainer. On Stan's death in June 1974, Mrs Fox, a racing enthusiast, had decided to keep the stable going. Denham had been with S & M Fox Investments for ten years.

Published stories that claim Stan Fox had taken a shine to me when I was working at the Denham stables in those early days, and that this was behind the 'call-up' in 1978, are way off the mark. I think I only met Mr Fox once, when I was working at the Denham stable in my stint in Sydney in the late 1960s. He would come to the stable now and then and walk around talking to the boys, asking them how this or that horse was going. As far as he was concerned I would have been just another face in the sea of employees who washed through the place over the years, just another strapper. I went about my business back then in a quiet sort of way, and when we talked in 1978 Mrs Fox had no memory at all of me being there in those earlier years.

* * *

I drove to Clareville after trackwork a day or two later and met Mrs Fox and Ken Ennever. We went through the horses they had in the stable, and she told me the reasons why Jack Denham was leaving. It is not for me to disclose those reasons or what I was told that day. The fact was, he was going, and there was an opportunity.

I had never met Millie Fox before that day. I had seen her at the races, of course, but never spoken to her. 'Why me?' I asked her, stumbling out some words about other people being better qualified. Mrs Fox said to me: 'Stan would have liked someone like you. You have a good reputation and you've done well since you came to Sydney. People speak well of you. I know he would have liked you.'

I recognised the offer for what it was. Here now was my opportunity to step into the big league as a private trainer. The Fox stable consisted mainly of home-bred horses, and I knew there wouldn't be instant success. It still put me into a big stable, big numbers. Turnover. On acceptance—and I didn't hesitate long before saying 'yes'—I had jumped from nine horses to more than 100, with sixty in work. It was another step up the ladder and, like those other strokes of fate that have punctuated my life with some regularity, it left me amazed. How was it that things kept falling into place?

I started my new life on 15 April 1978, wishing my mum had still been alive to see me get this chance, knowing how pleased she would have been. She had died twelve months earlier.

✖ ✖ ✖

Newspapers noted I was a 'despondent figure' (I never could disguise my disgust at losing!) on the first Randwick race day soon afterwards, after I had saddled up four Fox runners, Command Module, Smokey, Happy Way and Triumphant.

While Command Module ran a place, the others missed out. It was not exactly the start I had hoped for but a few days later, on 26 April, Smokey, by the sprinting sire Corinto, beat the 7/4 favourite So Considerate to win a staying handicap over two miles at Canterbury—and I was on my way.

The winners came in a more or less steady flow after that. When I had first accepted the position at Nebo Lodge, Mrs Fox told me I would be lucky to win races with the horses then on hand. I weeded out a lot of no-hopers, and initially cut the team at Nebo Lodge to about thirty horses to concentrate on the seventy-odd rising two year olds of the next season. Even so, in the first three months with Mrs Fox, we won twenty races and $70,000 in prize money, surpassing expectations.

With forty-two and a half winners from 217 starters, I finished sixth on the trainers' ladder (behind Tommy Smith) that first Sydney season in 1978–79. But on percentage of runners to winners, I was on top of the list at 19.9 per cent.

Eight months into the first season of my tenure at Nebo Lodge, a journalist asked me the question, 'Can you see yourself ever becoming the leading trainer in Sydney?'

I answered this way: 'There's this other bloke around called Smith, you know. But seriously, in around six or seven years I hope to be in a position to give him a run for his money. I know plenty have tried in the past—but that's the goal I have set myself.'

* * *

In November 1978, S & M Fox Investments was a big, big concern. When Mrs Fox, then seventy-nine, made the decision to cut back some years later, beginning from early 1983, she had three stallions and about 110 brood mares on the books. You can imagine the numbers of foals and yearlings—

every year there were about sixty-five yearlings to educate and get ready.

Millie Fox was a lovely person. I always thought that if an ordinary person could be 'royalty', then she was such a person. She was always gracious, never complained, was never difficult. She took her involvement in racing quietly, but with a genuine passion. She was a real lady.

Ken Ennever was secretary and manager of the Fox establishment and had been since the foundry days. He'd been with Stan Fox for years, way back to the days before Stan went into horses. Ken was a decent man, a very capable man, and we worked well together. As the seasons rolled along after that first morning at Clareville, we had a lot of fun . . . and won a lot of races.

Working exclusively with Mrs Fox's home-bred horses, I twice ran third in the trainers' premiership, behind Tommy Smith and Neville Begg (1981–82, 1982–83). We had a lot of enjoyment and considerable success with horses bred by the likes of Sir Dane, Bogan Road, Village Square, Purple Patch and Swashbuckler. The partnership lasted six years and in that time we won more than 300 races on metropolitan tracks and as many again on country and provincial tracks.

One memory, of many, is how, with an old character of a horse named More Mink, we almost beat the great Kingston Town at Rosehill one day. More Mink was a real personality horse, and one of ability, who placed in group races. He always had this slightly wild look in his eye, like 'I'm going to do something soon . . . I'm going to get you in a minute.' On this particular day, Malcolm Johnston got in front on the champion Kingston Town and when he thought he had the race won, dropped his hands. More Mink came swooshing down the outside and when they hit the line everyone went 'Whoooooohhhhh!' Malcolm nearly fell out of the saddle, and nobody knew who had won the race. Eventually the photo came down and Kingston Town had survived by an inch or so. Malcolm Johnston got a severe talking-to from the stewards, and plenty of publicity. It could have been worse: if he'd been beaten in those circumstances, the stewards would have had his guts for garters.

✖✖✖

The success gained with essentially home-bred stock was no doubt the reason behind my next *huge* break in training, when the world's most successful owner, Robert Sangster, took over Nebo Lodge—the fulfilment of an idea that stemmed originally from the Canadian businessman Bob Lapointe, Sangster's partner in the operation—and invited me to head it up.

This was pretty much right in line with the Mayfield-Smith story so far—an unexpected breakthrough. It was 1984, and Mrs Fox had been steadily reducing the operation as she had planned. It was a big cut, too, from the huge string that had been the S & M Fox operation to just one stallion (Command Module) and about fifteen brood mares. It was obvious things were on the way down at Nebo Lodge, and because of the developments there, headlines appeared in the newspaper that I was again 'going public' as a trainer. They were true.

It was at that precise moment that Bob Lapointe, head of the ARABS (Australian Racing and Breeding Stable) syndicate, appeared on the scene. Lapointe was a real racing enthusiast, owner of the champion mare Emancipation, and the man who had introduced Kentucky Fried Chicken and Pizza Hut to Australia, and who later added Sizzler to that list. He had the idea of putting together a big stable, but needed someone of Robert Sangster's stature to bring it off. On a yacht on Sydney Harbour one day, a plan was hatched between the two of them.

And so it was that, just at the stage when I was getting ready to go out the gate and be a little battling trainer again, with no stables, suddenly I was back in business, retained by two of the racing world's biggest owners to train for them, and at Nebo Lodge, where I was already comfortably installed with the Fox Investments team. The ARABS (51 per cent) and Robert Sangster (49 per cent) paid $2.3 million to buy Nebo Lodge, their partnership hailed as a new dynamic force in Australian racing. Until then, Sangster's operations had been mainly geared from Lindsay Park Stud in South Australia. Before long, Nebo Lodge underwent a $1 million facelift, which effectively turned it into a luxury motel for horses.

It was another one of those casual, chance things that have punctuated my life. A fellow named Les Young came around with Bob Lapointe to have a general yarn about the possibilities. If he could get Robert Sangster as a partner, Lapointe told me, they wanted me as trainer. I had never had any dealings with either Lapointe or Sangster. The main reason for the interest was my 'strike rate' as a trainer, the reasoning being that if I could succeed with the home-breds I had, then I would do even better with the sort of stock they could bring in.

And so my life changed again. From diverse threads we built a big, and successful, team. But it is a myth that it was the full weight of Robert Sangster's wealth that carried me all the way to the top. The stable, in fact, was very much a 'collective': Sangster's horses made up about 30 per cent, the remainder of the Fox horses 30 per cent—Bob Lapointe was in there too with the ARABS syndicate—and other owners made up another 30 per cent.

The Sangster presence brought an inevitable dash of

glamour to the whole operation. He was, after all, a citizen of the world who moved in rich company and high places. Via the stud syndicate, Sangster had a worldwide involvement in thoroughbred breeding and racing, his empire extending from England, France and Ireland to the United States, South Africa, New Zealand . . . and Australia. Funded by the Sangster family's English Pools monopoly, Robert had plunged into horseracing in the early 1970s when he linked up with the famous Irish trainer Vincent O'Brien.

As a successful horse trainer, part of the job involves dealing with some very high-flying people. I found that side of it hard. Sangster, to his credit, accepted me for what I was. The fact that I had never had an outward-going personality, and had spent most of my working hours with the horses, had left me with little time to 'cultivate' new owners or to indulge in the politics that goes with acquiring more horses. But the support of two men like Sangster and Lapointe enabled me to still pretty much run my 'natural race'. As a bloke raised in North Queensland, it was not easy for me to be anything other than genuine. Soft-sell bullshit was not my way. In my growing-up days up north, bullshit artists and skites were never much tolerated.

The fact is, bullshit happens in racing just as it does in other facets of life. There are trainers who tell people what they know those people want to hear. They paint as rosy a picture as possible. I have always had difficulty with that. I'd like to think that if people have any perception of me in the racing business, they see in me a degree of ability at the top level, and also that if they deal with me they're not going to be touched. So, getting into the 'glamorous' side of racing—and there is glamour when you have success at the highest level—wasn't easy for me. I'm not sure if I ever 'made it' in that way. I was just straightforward, and people seemed comfortable enough with that. In 1997, *Sunday Telegraph* racing writer Richard Zachariah observed in a lengthy article on my Flemington set-up: 'Racing is more than working the room. How else would the largely antisocial Jack Denham get a horse? Or an outsider like Brian Mayfield-Smith survive?' 'Yes, I am an outsider,' I told Zachariah in the course of that interview.

One bloke I had enjoyable dealings with, and with whom Maree and I forged a friendship, was then Prime Minister Bob Hawke, a man with the common touch, and a real racing enthusiast. With Bob the conversation was most often horses, but sometimes it was elephants too—and I'll admit that Maree and I gave the PM some earbashings on the subject of the ivory trade. We welcomed the Federal Government putting a ban on the importing of ivory into Australia (with the exception of antique ivory). I will always be grateful to Bob Hawke for allowing us to be a small part of this significant decision. I admired, too, Bob's stand against the decision to mine Coronation Hill, a decision which would lead to run-off damage to the wetlands of Kakadu National Park. It was a very brave position to adopt in the face of political and big business pressure.

* * *

Robert Sangster and Bob Lapointe were great owners. They never really interfered. As long as I kept them fully informed, they virtually left it to me. It was a big, big operation. Each morning the eighty to 100 Nebo Lodge horses in work would have to be marshalled via the lights across the traffic-choked James Ruse Drive to Rosehill Racecourse, tethered in batches of eleven. Walkie-talkies helped make it all work. I would be in the centre of the course, directing operations from the trainers' viewing stand; stable foreman Lewis Seib was back at Nebo; and my brother Noel would be on a third walkie-talkie at the Rosehill horse stalls, with Bill Farrow, a longtime employee of Nebo Lodge. Bill was there when I was a stablehand at Nebo Lodge back in 1969. He was an important part of my operation. He rode trackwork and straightened out a lot of difficult horses for me in those early days at Rosehill. It's been said that I'm not real good company early of a morning at the track. Probably it's true. There is so much to be done, all of it summed up in a basic philosophy: work your butt off, pay attention to detail, and have an intuitive feel for your horses and the work they need. At the track I'm focused, thinking, trying to get it right.

Back then, I laid down my philosophy as a horse trainer about both horses and people: 'The main rule,' I said, 'is that basically I must like the horse. And I will only train for people who have a good reputation in racing. I won't be associated with shady characters. If the owner hasn't got a very good character, then I won't train the horse, no matter how good it is. The system has been tightened up a lot in the past few years, so much so that trickery hardly ever works, although you will always get someone who slips through the net.'

Nebo Lodge, which became the centre of my world, grew into a state-of-the-art stable. And on a grand scale. It was as far removed from my beginnings back at Cannon Park Racecourse in Cairns as the earth is from the moon. At Nebo Lodge we had room for 110 horses. There were swimming pools, walking tracks—anything you needed to get horses fit. The main house had its own swimming pool; the staff were housed in a double-storey block of units. A racing journalist once described it this way: 'Glazed, manicured, press-buttoned, paved, landscaped, pot-planted and generally immaculate.' There was an entertainment lounge which overlooked a small parade ring, a woodchip exercise track, flowerbeds, landscaped paths, bowling-green lawns and cobblestone pavements. The value of the Nebo Lodge establishment, with Bob Lapointe and Robert Sangster on board, was conservatively estimated to be $6 million. My full-time stable staff numbered thirty-two, plus office staff to plough through the reams of paperwork.

At the peak of the operation we had 330 horses on the books, and 100 in work. Via a sideline I took up—learning to fly a helicopter—I would check every single horse, every week. In the main I enjoyed the instruction and the flying experience under my teacher, Chris Townsend of Hoxton Park. But I never did get my licence, although I got plenty of solo hours up. The first time I climbed aboard and we took off over the freeway at Hoxton Park, I almost shat myself. We were in this tiny little thing with no doors on the side, feeling like we were going to drop out of the sky. I thought then, if this bloody thing gets safely back on the ground, you won't find me within 100 yards of one of these again! But I kept coming back, because it was a challenge. I just didn't have the time to do the study. After my long days I'd pick up one of the books at night—and they're bloody complex things—and after about two pages, I'd be nodding off. But I ended up flying solo without killing myself.

I went close once, though. On a solo flight one day when turning from base leg to final approach and landing, I made the mistake of turning the aircraft with the foot pedal instead of the cyclic (steering control). When I looked down at my airspeed indicator it showed about five knots! A bolt of fear went through my body like an electrical current, from my toes to the roots of my hair. I'm dead!, I thought. But my training came to my rescue—as my instructor had always said it would—and somehow I sorted it out and made it to the ground intact.

Of a Thursday, I'd do my tour of inspection, flying to

Mrs Fox's property, Coolamon Park, at St Mary's, then to Belmont Park at Windsor and on to Muskoka Farm at Wiseman's Ferry.

As a private trainer for S & M Fox I was reconciled to the fact that the most I could achieve was the status of Sydney's third most successful trainer, because of the standard of the horses I had to work with. With the arrival of Sangster and Lapointe—and with them the services of renowned breeding authority Les Young, who looked after Bob Lapointe's interests—the playing field had changed dramatically. I knew that someone was going to take over from T.J. Smith one day, and I wanted it to be me. Now, the chance was there. I had arrived at the gates, and for me it was a case of put up or shut up. This was going to be the best chance that I would ever get, and I wasn't going to be denied. I went into 'overdrive'.

Chapter Twelve

The Day I Beat T.J. Smith

I had always promised myself that one day I would square up with T.J. Smith for what he had tried to do when I first brought Tiger Town to Sydney in 1978. On the day that I clinched the 1985–86 trainers' premiership with ninety-nine winners, ending Smith's thirty-three-year reign, there was a great deal of satisfaction deep down, I can tell you. Smith, who had had 792 starters that season to my 654, finished second on ninety-five-and-a-half winners. The bounty of the season included the winning of twenty-four group or listed events, including three Group 1 races: the Sydney Cup, the AJC Sires Produce and the Rawson Stakes.

I was happy to have it done. The endless speculation—would I beat Smith, or wouldn't I?—had irritated me through that season. Later, I told one journalist:

> Let's just get in and do it without all this talking. One thing I can't stand, if you'll excuse the expression, is piss and windbags.

I'd rather just get on with the job. It gives me the pip at times. You pick up a paper and it's 'so and so is edging closer and I'll do this or that' . . . it's so childish. Don't get me wrong. That doesn't mean I'm not super-competitive or positive about what I'm doing, but I like to do it in a quiet sort of way. I can't stand anyone shoving anything down my throat.

Tommy Smith and I never, ever spoke, so you couldn't say we had blues or anything like that. We just never spoke. A couple of times I was on the same table as him at luncheons and there would be general conversation going on. I never got involved in it with him. I thought, we never speak outside the room, so why speak here?

On the day I knocked him off his perch, I thought he showed a distinct lack of class. In a circumstance like that you might have expected him to come up and at least say 'Well done', even though he would have been hurting after all those years at the top. He went down in my estimation with his silence. Smith was a very great trainer—and I'll never be as good as him—but on that final day of the season I thought, if this bloke has really got what it takes inside, he'll have the guts to come up and say 'Well done', even if he picks his moment from a publicity point of view. He didn't come near me.

It had been an exciting finish. Going into the last day Smith trailed me by seven-and-a-half wins, and the racecourse was buzzing when horses from his stable won the first four races at Randwick. My only mild disappointment on the day was not to have trained the winner that would have brought me up to 100 for the season.

In the aftermath Smith never acknowledged my achievement in the media, in any shape or form. Instead there was always the excuse that he was beaten by some sort of international 'conglomerate'. That was shit. What he failed to mention was that one-third of the horses we had were

Mrs Fox's home-breds, another one-third were fairly cheap buys. Sure, in his first year Robert Sangster bought quite well, but after that he didn't buy as many. People had a perception of Sangster running around filling up the stable with all these top-priced yearlings. It wasn't the case. He moved into putting horses he had bred into the stable rather than buying a whole lot more. Which was fair enough. Marauding came out of that policy, though the champion stayer Marooned was one brought out from overseas.

But, consider this point: in the three years that we were the leading stable, not *once* was our stable in the top five yearling buyers at any sale. T.J. Smith had had forty years to establish himself; he had the game tied up. I think his attitude to me was just sour grapes. Fact was, I was a nobody, from nowhere. I wasn't some racing man's son or brother, or from some born-to-rule racing family in Sydney. That made it worse from his point of view.

It was the problem that Smith had to deal with and it seemed he couldn't rise above his feelings. It gave me some satisfaction, I suppose, that his reaction showed how much being beaten had hurt him. He just couldn't bring himself to acknowledge what I had achieved.

In life what you manage to achieve externally doesn't necessarily add up to much *inside* you. Success doesn't all of a sudden make you the nicest bloke or the best character around. Sure, lots of people want to know someone like T.J. Smith. But often there's another motive—a pressman wanting to get a story, a jockey chasing rides, staff seeking a job, a breeder wanting to have his horse in the leading trainer's stable to promote the stock. It's the way the world works. At my end the only positive comment I have to offer on the late 'T.J.' is that he was a great horse trainer.

There was some whingeing about how unlucky Tulloch Lodge (Smith stable headquarters) had been, particularly at

This is about as early as it gets in the Mayfield-Smith photo album—with my mum, Mabel, in Hobart, where I was born in May 1947.

A kid with a startled expression and a koala—a pic taken in my early years at Lone Pine Koala Sanctuary in Brisbane. Even then, I loved animals.

I suspect every country youngster has a photo or two like this in the family collection. It's me, bareback aboard Duchess in the backyard of our house in Mason Street, Stratford, Cairns.

Sport was always what I liked best about school—and cricket was high on that list. This is the end-of-season shot of the under-14s at Mt Carmel Christian Brothers College, Charter Towers, about 1960. I'm third from the right, front row—opening bowler for the under-14s that year.

If you look *real* closely at this photo, you'll see that the bloke second from the left in the middle row has a plaster cast on his left leg. It's me—in the Mt Carmel under nine-stone rugby league side, but nursing a broken leg. Football took quite a toll on me, due to injuries at school.

Left: Here's a snap taken at Victoria River Downs Station in the Northern Territory—a vast place of around 13,000 square kilometres, and home to 70,000 head of cattle during the time I was there.

Below: I revelled in the freedom of my early days as a stockman, roaming around among the big cattle stations. This faded shot is from Kamilaroi Station up in the Gulf country, and I'm standing in front of the van driven by a hawker who used to visit from time to time. His arrival was always a big event at these lonely stations.

Above: The place where it all began—the caravan parked under the Moreton Bay fig at Cannon Park Racecourse, Cairns—my home when I first became a racehorse trainer. Figs from the tree would plop onto the roof, and the canvas for my 'add-on' never lasted too long once the northern wet set in.

The trainer and his (one) horse. My mother took this photo of me with Gay Meld, the filly that became my first winner when she bolted in at Mareeba one Saturday afternoon in April 1971. The photograph carries the inscription 'Masterpiece of photography by Mater'.

Here I am in famous company—with the legendary US champion Secretariat, in Kentucky. In 1985, Robert Sangster and Bob Lapointe sent Maree and me on a study tour of world racing which took in England, Ireland, France and the US.

This was a proud day at Rosehill—a presentation from the Sydney Turf Club, via chairman Jim Fleming (right), after I had won the trainer's premiership of 1985–86.

Below: The Robert Sangster-bred colt Marauding, galloping before the 1987 Golden Slipper.

I had enjoyable dealings with Lester Piggott (left), one of the all-time great English jockeys. His son-in-law, William Haggas, spent some time with us out here, learning the ropes before heading back to England to take up training. This photo was taken at Warwick Farm.

I rate Jim Cassidy the best jockey of my experience, and the partnership has been a fruitful one over the years, despite some well-publicised 'difficulties'. Here we are at the Epsom Training Centre, Mordialloc, with handy sprinter Slave Trade.

Left: Maree and I cut the cake on our wedding day in 1985. We were married in Strathfield, Sydney—and the reception was held back at Nebo Lodge. I consider myself very lucky to have found someone like Maree, who shares my interests—and is as passionate about wildlife as I am.

This was a wonderful and memorable day—with Maree and the Golden Slipper Trophy at Rosehill after Marauding won the big race in 1987.

In 1989, I travelled to Japan, along with some notable racing men, as a guest of the Japan Racing Association. At the track in Tokyo we lined up for a photo—left to right: John Kelso, Reg Inglis, Treeve Williams, Bob Lapointe and me.

Prime Minister Bob Hawke, a keen racing man and a friend, invited us several times to Kirribilli House. On this day, Maree and I were joined by her mum and dad, John and Val Fitzgerald.

Kwai River, Botswana, was the first camp we stayed in when our 'African Adventure' began, back in 1987. It's a special place—one of the most beautiful in all Africa, and the photo captures my first contact with wild elephants on the ground.

This was a sad sight … a bad day. This female elephant lying in the Ewaso Ngiro River on Ivan Tomlinson's ranch had a severely infected foot. It was decided she should be put out of her misery.

Right: Under Kenyan law the ivory has to be removed from a slain elephant—and conveyed to the Kenyan Wildlife Service. There was no joy for any of us in the events of this day.

Below: Meeting one of the young inhabitants of Daphne Sheldrick's famous elephant orphanage, outside Nairobi. It's 1988.

With one of the rhino at Western Plains Zoo.

Pictured with a couple of good-looking acquaintances at Tipperary Downs, businessman Warren Anderson's private wildlife sanctuary in the Northern Territory. The year is 1992.

With Gus, the male cheetah at the Western Plains Zoo, Dubbo, NSW. The photo is from 1993, the year that Maree and I became involved in supporting the zoo's work—notably the black rhino program.

It was here, in 1996, at a campsite in Ivan Tomlinson's property outside Nanyuki, that we decided we'd break off the African 'experiment' and head back to Australia to reassess our lives. This was a special place—dominated by that remarkable hanging rock. The baboons would scamper straight up its sheer face.

This is as far as you can go on the African continent—to Cape Agulhas on the southernmost tip. In 1995–96, we travelled all the way from the equator down to that deepest southern point.

With kids from a Masai village—on tribal land
near the Masai Mara reserve.

Wayne Hamilton (left) and his wife Tracey were great and generous friends to us in Africa. We first met them when they ran the Flight Centre agency in Eastgardens, Sydney. Their kindness in putting us up in Johannesburg added special enjoyment to our 1995–96 trek. Now and then on our travels they joined us on safaris. Here Wayne and I pose before a well-stocked camp bar in the Okavango Delta.

At Lewa (the word means 'drunk' in Swahili) Downs near Mount Kenya with two cheetah from Mombasa Zoo, that were being readied for return to the wild. They were doing well.

Below: Tracking lions in the Okavango Delta, 1999.

Maree and I take a break during a walking safari in the Okavango Delta, 1999.

Our four-wheel drive—seriously bogged in the Moremi Game Reserve. It took one and a half hours to dig it out—and the whole time we were looking over our shoulders in case something wandered out of the bush.

With Jock, the part Staffordshire bull terrier who does his best to run the Mayfield-Smith house in Melbourne. He was named after South Africa's most famous canine, Jock of the Bushveld, a tough little Staffordshire terrier who is said to have fought off baboons, lions and crocodiles as he travelled the 19th century trade routes with his master, Percy Fitzpatrick.

a late-season meeting at which the stable won a double, lost two other races in photo finishes and another, the STC Winter Cup, on protest to one of my horses, Bold Endeavour. I replied this way: 'The first horse I ran in Sydney, Tiger Town, lost an Epsom by a nose, yet it was an eternity away from winning—just as a three-and-a-half deficit is.'

Much was made back then of my achievement in beating Tommy Smith, who had come from a working-class background himself to knock out Maurice McCarten in the 1951–52 trainers' premiership. I was five years old when that happened. It was noted that I had first featured on the Sydney premiership list in 1976–77, finishing twenty-third with six metropolitan wins, 121 behind Smith. The following year I had moved up to tenth, with fourteen-and-a-half wins. In 1982 and 1983, I was third; then sixth in 1984 and 1985. Now, I had done it . . . It was a proud time for me. During the victory celebrations at Nebo Lodge, I showed the gathered Sydney media a letter I had received from Robert Sangster. It read:

> Dear Brian,
> Many congratulations on winning the premiership in Sydney. The realisation of this goal by Nebo Lodge ahead of schedule is truly an accomplishment to be proud of.
>
> For the past two years you have been telling me of the excellence of the staff you have at Nebo Lodge and this has been very apparent on all my visits to the stables. I am sure that your enormous success this year is due in part to the extremely good team you have put together.
>
> I would like you to pass on my thanks to all the staff for a job very well done and I look forward to seeing you on my next trip to Australia, in the spring.

I can tell you, it gave me a very great deal of satisfaction when I received the 1985–86 trainers' trophy from STC chairman Jim Fleming. In my acceptance speech, I told the crowd it was one of the proudest days of my life:

> I had two ambitions when I came to Sydney ten years ago—one was to win the Melbourne Cup, the other to win the Sydney trainers' premiership. I am a man who strives for perfection and this victory is more pleasant for me in that not only did I beat Tom [Smith] on wins but I had twenty more seconds and twenty-one more thirds and won more prize money in Sydney with 138 fewer runners than the Smith stable. I feel the victory is complete.

To win the premiership was a wonderful thing to achieve, creating a great feeling of inner euphoria, but I told anyone who bothered to ask that I had no ambition to chase Smith's record of thirty-three straight premierships, that life held other, different challenges for me. For sure I didn't want to stay in Sydney and chase the premiership every year, like a dog chasing its tail. But I went on to win the premiership three years straight, and in my mind that was enough to dispel any perception that I was a 'one-hit wonder'.

For a time I toyed with international ambitions—of taking horses from my stable to the US on a regular basis. That was sort of in line with the reality that I am a bit of a bloody dreamer. Nothing came of this one, but it was another thrust at breaking away from the 'mundane'. It was in the same spirit as my later decision to give up everything and go to Africa, with people looking at me and thinking, what the HELL is he doing? I have dreamed my big dreams since I was a little fella in North Queenland, accepting that you have to start with a dream to create a reality.

I really believe you have to have dreams in your life, things you seek that might be just beyond fingertip reach. The problem to contend with is that once you *reach* that dream, things are never the same. The two premierships that followed meant a lot too—but not quite as much as that first one. You have achieved your dream and now there is nothing there—just an emptiness. In some ways it is better if we have dreams that are *always* just out of reach, giving us the impetus to continue striving and reaching out (although I can tell you, there was no emptiness when I knocked over T.J. Smith that first time . . .).

I don't think I'll ever change on that score. For me the pursuit of something different is the very essence of life. Africa was about that, as were other things I have done. I believe you just have to experience as much of life as you can. I always have a sense of time running out. The seeking of new experiences is about a restlessness inside, on the one hand, but it's a pursuit of inner peace as well. I doubt it will ever leave me, to be honest.

* * *

I find Gai Waterhouse, the daughter of my old rival Tommy Smith, completely different to her father. I take people as I find them—and I think a whole lot of Gai. She's a lovely person, and I admire greatly what she has achieved—and under great difficulties at times. She's a friendly, natural person who will go out of her way to say, 'G'day'. She has done outstandingly well—and good luck to her.

CHAPTER THIRTEEN

Some Horses I Have Known

As you may have gathered from the start, this is not a book about horseracing. My only motivation for telling my story was to spotlight Africa—its animals, its problems, its delights. For the fact was, and is, that my life changed profoundly when I discovered that amazing country. Primarily, I wanted to share the experience in the words of my own travels there, and if it happened that the book could help in a small way—in any money it might generate to help endangered species or in any education it could provide—then all the better. For me, the discovery of Africa added meaning and purpose to a life which had, to that point, bumped along, although not uninterestingly, taken this way and that by the many chance events that complemented the hard work I put in.

But the fact of my life, of course, is that much of it has been spent around racehorses—wonderful, noble animals, and each one of them as different to the next as we humans are to one another. It would be remiss of me if some of their stories weren't told in these pages. So, here are some slices of racing life, most of them from the days when I was at the top of the heap, Sydney's leading trainer. Here you will meet some of the horses that have stuck in my mind for their deeds and their character over the years.

I'll start with one of the best yarns. It concerns not only a very fine horse indeed, but it also drives home—more powerfully than pretty much any other story I can think of—just how much the element of chance has dictated the major events of my life.

In 1987, I won the coveted Golden Slipper Stakes at Rosehill with Robert Sangster's imposing colt Marauding (Sir Tristram–Biscalowe). Marauding had only one race in the spring of 1986, and was beaten by a nose by Maizcay in race record time in the Silver Slipper Stakes. I spelled him before bringing him back for the Coca-Cola Classic, which he won in course record time at Newcastle. It was apparent then that he was special.

I knew he was a great Slipper chance, and my wish was to give him one more run before the Golden Slipper, but not the week before the race, because I felt that was too close, that it would rob him of his speed and that he would get too far back, and the race would get away from him. My preference by a long way was to run him in the Todman Slipper Trial, two weeks before the Classic.

After the Newcastle win, I rang Robert Sangster in his Isle of Man office. I explained what I wanted to do with Marauding and why—and there was silence at the other end of the line. 'Brian, we've got a problem,' said Sangster. 'Colin Hayes [the great South Australian-based trainer who was also training for Sangster] wants to run Kaapstad in the Todman too, and I won't have my two good colts running against each other.'

I stuck to my guns. 'This horse will win the Slipper,' I told him, 'but he won't win it if he runs the week before.'

There was another pause, and then Sangster's voice: 'Oh, well—there's only one way to solve this. We'll flip a coin.'

'What?!' I said. 'Do you mean here and now . . . over the phone?'

'Yep,' he said.

'That's a bit unusual, isn't it?' I said.

'What do you want—heads or tails?' said Robert Sangster, 20,000 kilometres away. When I hesitated, he pushed it along: 'Call it, Brian.' He wanted to get on with it. Sangster had his bloodstock manager, Mark Glyer, with him in the office, and Glyer was the one charged with the duty of flipping the coin. Complicating matters was the fact that he was a part-owner in the lease on Kaapstad!

Usually I call 'heads', but for some reason I switched. 'Tails,' I said. There was silence, and then some muffled talking in the background. I could hear Mark's voice: 'It's a tail, Robert,' and Sangster was back on the phone.

'Okay, Brian,' he said. 'You can run—and I'll have to ring Colin and tell him that Kaapstad can't.'

I put the phone down, a little stunned. Thirty seconds later it rang again and when I picked it up I heard the three quick beeps of a long-distance call. I knew who it was. There was a sort of apologetic cough and then a voice said, 'Colin?'

'No, Robert,' I said. 'It's Brian here. I think you've rung the wrong number.' Sangster had fumbled the call. Even for a man of the world like Robert Sangster, it was no easy thing to ring a respected trainer and friend and tell him that he may well have just lost his chance of winning the Golden Slipper—on the toss of a coin.

The story says quite a lot about Robert Sangster. I always found him a very fair man—but he was a gambler as well, a man who loved a bet. Solving a major dilemma in the way he did was a very natural solution to him.

As history had it, Kaapstad didn't run in the big race (the Golden Slipper) anyway. He was sold to new owners a week or so before. And Marauding won his pre-Slipper hit-out, a fortnight before, quite comfortably—and then came in with a barnstorming finish in the Golden Slipper to beat Lygon Arms by a nose and win $500,000 first-prize money. The manner of his victory absolutely vindicated my opinion that if he had been forced to race just one week out from the Slipper, he wouldn't have had the necessary speed to be competitive.

People said later that Marauding would have lasted longer if he hadn't run in the Slipper. But he was such a big, strong horse as a two year old—a real handful—that we decided to educate him so we could stay ahead of him a bit. The colt had phenomenal speed—and the fact was, Robert Sangster really wanted to win a Slipper. So that's what we went for.

We knew all along we were on borrowed time with the horse. We had X-rayed his legs and the print had revealed a tiny chip in one knee, and another under the joint in the other leg, which vet Percy Sykes said had been there for quite some time. When he came out of his box cold, he would always take a couple of funny little steps; once he warmed up and worked he was fine, and fine when he pulled up, too. I have no doubt the decision was the right one, to capitalise on his natural speed and ability early. One day the problem was going to catch up with him. And it did. He had a hard run from a wide barrier in the Sire's Produce in his next start, finishing third behind Snippets and Sky Chase, and pulled up a bit short. We immediately spelled him. When he came back, the soft tracks of that particular spring didn't suit him. The decision was made to retire him to stud, where he went on to sire a couple of Golden Slipper winners himself.

⁂

The imported stayer Marooned (Mill Reef–Short Rations), bought cheaply by Robert Sangster, was a cripple, basically, but with phenomenal galloping ability. His track sectional times and race sectional times were far superior to even the top sprinters. But he had this problem in his near front leg, which was crooked: it slanted out at an angle from the knee instead of going straight down. When he galloped, he would swing the leg, putting intense pressure on because he was such a fast horse. After trackwork on at least three occasions, he pulled up deadset lame on three legs. Each time you'd think, this time he's finished, but by taking it easy on him, swimming him for a few days . . . he'd come good. Then the pattern would be repeated. I knew the problem would catch up with him one day, and it did.

He won the Sydney Cup for me in 1988, pulled up sore, and I immediately spelled him. When we brought him back he was getting so much arthritis around his joints that it was just too uncomfortable for him. We retired him, ending the short, sweet saga of Marooned.

When he came to me he hadn't had a start for nine months, no barrier trial or anything. In his first run, in Canterbury welter, he missed the jump by three lengths—then flew home at the end to get within three-quarters of a length of the winner. One stride past the post he was in front, so fast did he finish. For his next start we jumped him up to the Canterbury Cup, and he got beaten by a nose after being held up in traffic on the home turn. Once again, he 'flew' home. I nominated him for the Sydney Cup and, because he was basically a welter horse, he was given only 49.5 kilograms.

Before the Cup I entered him in two penalty-free group races—the Manion Cup (Rosehill) and the Chairman's Handicap (Randwick)—and he won both of them in a breeze. If there is any such thing as a handicapping certainty, then he was it in the Cup. By all rights he should have had fifty-four kilograms or so, but because we had placed him right he was in on the 'postage stamp' of 49.5.

Before the Cup there was some mischievous talk circulated that the horse was lame again. The stories were garbage. The papers buzzed with speculation about whether the horse was sound, or whether he had gone wrong. The timing was deeply suspicious and it all gained momentum with a major headline a couple of days before the race, precipitating a vet's examination which would decide whether he could start. AJC Chief Steward John Shreck ordered the veterinary test, following reports that Marooned had a filling in a leg. If you were inclined to cynicism—and after being in racing all these years, of course I'm not!—you would almost think that someone was conspiring to get him out of the Cup.

Anyway, these two vets came around and we gave him some work, and they were quite happy. I said to them straight: 'This horse came out here with legs that were less than perfect. They are no different now to what they were when he won the Manion and the Chairman's. So what's all the fuss about?'

'Well, we're just doing our job,' one of them said. I sensed they knew what was going on.

'Fair enough,' I said.

Marooned went out two days later and won the 3200 Metres Cup easily at 13/8 on. It was little more than a track gallop for him. Afterwards Jim Cassidy declared him the best horse he had ridden—better even than Kiwi. 'It's just like driving a nice big motor car,' said Cassidy of the horse. Marooned, described by one newspaper as 'appearing to be going only three-quarter pace', gave Cassidy an armchair ride.

Robert Sangster had had a very good run on the punt leading up to this race. It had been a successful autumn carnival for me and some of my winners had been Robert's horses, including English Mint at 66/1, which he had backed each way. Heading into Sydney Cup day, he was winning $124,000, quite a bit of it from leading bookmaker Dominic Beirne. Robert challenged Dominic: 'Give me even money Marooned for the $124,000 and I'll give you a chance to get the lot.' Dominic Beirne didn't hesitate—and took the bet.

***

Fate (again!) played a hand in the story of Brindisi (Village Square–Miss Italy), my first Group 1 winner. When I first started racing him I thought he was a nice enough horse, not real big, with some ability. But when he got beaten in a moderate race at Kembla Grange one day, I thought, this bloke isn't anything out of the box; I'll put him on the market. I put $10,000 on him and a bloke from up the coast was interested, but wanted to haggle. He did his utmost to beat me down to $8000. In the end, I said to him: 'Mate, I'm not in the horse-trading business. Ten is the price. You pay $10,000 or the horse is not for sale.'

Still he persisted. 'I'll give you $8000, now.'

'Forget it,' I said.

So I kept Brindisi and he made steady improvement. Within eight starts or so he won a Canterbury Cup, and half a dozen starts later, the 1980 $120,000 AJC Metropolitan. I was lucky. He was part of a process at Nebo Lodge at the time when Mrs Fox was reducing her string and we were trying to cut the list—get rid of the lesser animals, if I can put it that way. Brindisi was small, and by an ordinary sire (Village Square), and he went onto the list of those to go. Luckily for me, he got a reprieve. And I did, too. I would have looked a nice goose if the bloke had taken him and he'd gone on to win big races.

He won the Metrop as a 40/1 outsider. Rodney Quinn, a jockey who never used to say a lot, rode him in a gallop on the cinders track at Rosehill on the Saturday (the Metrop was on the next Monday). When he came back in, Quinn said: 'That was good work. I don't know what price this horse is in the Metrop, but on that, he'll take a lot of beating.'

Fifty-year-old Ray Selkrig rode him on the big day and he just rounded them up from the turn, skipped past them over the rise, said, 'See you later' and won running away. There's a great photo of him passing the post, with all four feet off the ground.

It was a special day for me—my first major group winner for Mrs Fox, and her first since the days of Purple Patch. The Metropolitan, in those days anyway, was a time-honoured race. To win it was a great thing for me—and especially so at Randwick, which has always been my favourite track. That day, I thought back to Tiger Town and how he'd got beaten by a cigarette-paper width at my first attempt at winning one of the big races at Randwick. And I thought back to Cairns, nine years before, when I'd been slogging around with a couple of scrubbers. It had been quite a journey, to arrive at the top of the mountain at a place like Randwick with all its tradition. That track to me is what a racecourse should be—a big, spacious track, giving horses their chance. My preference is for big tracks, and my horses always perform better on those.

✖✖✖

Handy Proverb (Twig Moss–Summer Crest) provides special memories for me. He won two Derbies for me (VRC and Queensland) and was almost a triple Derby winner. In the AJC Derby of 1986, he was unlucky enough to run into the champion New Zealander, Bonecrusher. And he was unlucky in the way that race was run, too. Bonecrusher had a lovely run, and at the 600 metres the jockey moved him out so he could go forward when he wanted to. Handy Proverb, by contrast, had a bad draw and was always back, and wide. He virtually had to make a run from the 800 metres crossing, around the whole field. Bonecrusher was in front of him, and he went up with the jockey hardly moving on him over the rise. Handy Proverb chased him hard, and for a few strides looked as though he was going to get him, but Bonecrusher lifted and held him off—so denying him a third Derby.

Handy Proverb's wins in the VRC Derby and the Queensland Derby—a race in which he chopped almost three seconds off the previous record—plus the St Leger and the Grand Prix, stamped him as very special. I wouldn't say he was a champion, but he was an outstanding, staying three year old and was voted as such in his year.

As a matter of fact I don't believe I have ever (yet!) got to train a genuine 'champion', a word which is thrown around rather too cheaply. Over the years I have had a lot of really outstanding horses, but never one which I would term a champion—a Manikato, a Kingston Town, a Dulcify. The thought that one of those might be just around the corner is what keeps us all going.

✻ ✻ ✻

Rare Form (Bogan Road–On Her Toes) was a big, raw-boned horse and a terrific galloper who had the distinction of beating the mighty Kingston Town on a day on which all the other riders in the field seemed out to get 'The King'. It happened in the Chelmsford Stakes at Randwick at a time when Kingston Town was sweeping all before him. As I said, it seemed as if all the jocks were riding to get Kingston Town beaten that day and when they approached the 700 metres, they had him boxed up tight on the fence. While all this was going on, John Duggan on Rare Form whipped around the field and skipped him well clear of the pack over the rise. By the time the penny dropped and the other jockeys stopped worrying about Kingston Town, Rare Form was four or five lengths in front. And he was the sort of horse that, once he got a break, he wouldn't stop—even if his run ended, he'd still keep plugging. With the chase on, Kingston Town at 11/4 on finally got some room, but by that time the bird had flown. The champion chased valiantly and took some ground off my bloke, but never looked like catching him. He ended up fourth, with Gurner's Lane second and Artist Man third. Rare Form won a Hobartville and the Canterbury Guineas, and played the giant-killer on another day when he beat the champion mare Emancipation in the All-Aged Stakes—but I guess that day at Randwick was his great one. I rate Kingston Town the best horse I have ever seen. He could mix his distances, he beat some very good horses along the way, and he could extend a winning run—ten, twelve wins on the trot, and against the best around.

* * *

Late Show (Purple Patch–Folies Bergere) was beaten at places like Hawkesbury and Kembla Grange in his first few runs, but even on those days was showing a glimpse of something special. I thought, this horse is going to do something; he's too good a mover not to be any good, and he'll show it when he gets over a bit of ground. After his first four starts, as the distances of his races increased, he started to put it together. In the end, he grew into a genuinely outstanding stayer, winner of a Canterbury Cup, a Rawson Stakes, and the Sydney Cup of 1985. On the day he won the Cup he was the only Australian-bred horse in the race. There was one European horse in the race, and all the rest were New Zealand-bred. The fact that it was a wet track helped the cause—Late Show loved the wet. But it wasn't just that. He was a bloody good stayer on any ground, with a beautiful action, and on Cup day Neil Campton rode him quietly as we had agreed to do—very quietly—and then just swept by them in the straight. He was a darned good horse, with this lovely long sweeping action. Late Show was the first horse I ever started in a 3200 metres race. I did not seek advice on his preparation; I did it myself and was proud when he won the race.

***

Riverina Charm (Sir Tristram–Country Charm) came to me after having been given time in New Zealand on hilly paddocks owing to the fact that she had very poor conformation in her front legs. She had her first two starts for New Zealand trainer Laurie Laxton, winning first up, and on the potential shown in the two runs was sent to me to prepare for the good fillies races in Australia. She was owned by Robert Sangster, Peter and Phil Vella, Norman Carlyon and F.A. Krishnan. The stroke of good fortune (in her being sent across to Australia) gave me probably the best filly I ever trained. She remains the only filly to win the Canterbury Guineas–Rosehill Guineas double—both Group 1 events—and for good measure she won the Thousand Guineas (also Group 1) at Caulfield as well. She was always a challenge to train because of her bad legs and narrow conformation. In fact she was footsore before *both* Guineas victories, but won anyway. I recall Robert Sangster coming to the stable on the Thursday before the Rosehill Guineas. When he asked me about her, I replied she was 'great'—and at almost the same moment she walked out of her stable lame in the off-hind foot! He looked at me. I looked at him . . . I looked at her, then back at Robert. I was momentarily stuck for words. However, Robert was used to the vagaries of horses and racing and merely wished me 'good luck'. Two days later, notwithstanding the problem, she won the Rosehill Guineas. She also won the Hill Stakes (weight for age), the Edward Manifold Stakes (Group 2), and then went back to New Zealand and won the Air New Zealand Stakes at WFA for Laurie Laxton which, all things considered, was very fitting.

※※※

Magic Flute (Adraan–Ballet Dress) was a real quality filly, a sweet mover. She won the Widden Stakes as a two year old, the Reisling Slipper Trial, the AJC Keith Mackay Stakes and went on to win the Caulfield Thousand Guineas (a Group 1 race) and the Light Fingers Stakes (Group 3). Mike Willesee was looking for high-quality fillies at this time and took a shine to her. Eventually he bought her from the Swetenham Stud for a 'hell of a lot of money'. She promptly rewarded him by winning the Doncaster Handicap (Group 1) and the Queensland Guineas (Group 3). In her last couple of runs she wasn't at her best on rain-affected going, and after her fifth in the Elders Handicap (Group 1), she was retired to stud. Magic Flute had her beginning in racing when she was selected as a yearling by David Coles in Adelaide for Robert Sangster. Whenever I have been gauging quality in a filly in the years since, I think of her as the 'measuring stick'.

※※※

Winter's Dance (Bogan Road–Rhondelle) was one of the first good horses I had for Mrs Fox, but she had really ordinary joints. She was pinfired, had everything done that could be done in those days to help, but still she struggled. We gave her plenty of time, deciding not to race her as a two year old, even though she was showing outstanding ability on the track. I was so concerned about her legs I wouldn't even barrier trial her, fearing she might break down under the extra pressure.

When she was three, I decided to put her in a race, to see if she could at least win *one* for us. In a Gosford maiden in 1980, she raced four and five deep all the way, won easily—and ran faster time than the higher class races on the day. Somehow, and despite our concerns, her joints 'held together', and she went on to win her next six races, and emerge as favourite for the Stradbroke Handicap of that year as an unbeaten three-year-old filly.

But she had a gutbuster of a run the week before the Stradbroke, and that buggered her for the big race. In a 1200 metres group race, the Katies Cup, she missed the start and came from second-last to beat horses like Bemboka Yacht, Ducatoon, Turf Ruler and Hit It Benny—a sensational effort. Mick Dittman, one of the more punishing riders around, rode her—and it was Mick's vigour that got her home. But the run took its toll, and she raced dismally the next week. Winter's Dance came back, though, and won races like the Ajax Stakes (Rosehill) and the Tramway Handicap (Randwick). She was an outstanding sprinting mare.

***

Perhaps the horses that stick most in my mind are those that put in *every* run. I've had a few like that. Big Dreams (Habituate–Free As A Cloud) was an old favourite. He never won a Group 1 race, though he was placed in a hell of a lot of them. But he just kept putting in; he was always in there with a *chance* of winning.

Colour Page (Blue and Gold–Doll Tearsheet) was like that

too, a tough, genuine animal. He wasn't top of the ladder, but no one had told him that. He just did his best every time he went out there. Horses like that are noble, genuine, courageous animals. He was a big favourite of mine, although he seemed to be always just missing out in the big races. His stablemate Magic Flute knocked him off in the Doncaster of 1988, beat him by a neck—and Handy Proverb beat him in the Gloaming Stakes. He ran second in an Epsom Handicap. But he had his share of wins, too: a Prime Minister's Cup, Sandown Cup, Coongy Handicap, Queen Elizabeth Stakes. With a touch of luck he would have been right up there instead of being rated 'very handy'. He was one of those horses that you knew was going to do something every time he went onto the track. If he raced disappointingly, you knew for sure that there was something physically wrong with him.

Oliver Twist (Alex Nuryev–Honey Bridge), who is in my stable as I write this book, is a very similar type of horse. No one has told him he's not quite top-flight. He just gives his best every time he's saddled up. And so, too, Tiger Town (Royal Rocket–My Sharyn)—a very unlucky horse, but a tough horse who never put in a bad one. He answered the call every time I put him out there.

The funny thing about Colour Page was that he was a *very* ordinary trackworker. Race day was his speciality. It's remarkable how some horses are like that, although there are plenty more the other way—'morning glories' that are flash on the track, but don't produce in a race. That's all about mental pressure and physical pressure. Such horses may have all the natural ability in the world, but in the strain of competition, when the mind games are on, they can't cope, and they fall short of expectations. Just like we humans.

CHAPTER FOURTEEN

I Did It My Way

Punters, being the breed they are, search endlessly for the 'secrets' that will unearth winners for them. I'd love to be able to provide all the answers by unveiling those secrets in the pages of this book. But I'm afraid, after twenty-eight years as a trainer, I'm not that much help. People don't back horses second-up, won't back horses that break into a sweat, only back horses which are showing rib definition, etc., etc., etc. There are myriad theories at any racetrack. But my experience is that you can come up with every single theory in the world about what to look for in a horse when you go to the races, and most likely something which defies all the accepted wisdom will then come along and knock you off.

A lot of horses look well, look fit and are expected to run well—and don't. Conversely, you'll see a horse come into the enclosure all stirred up, and break into a muck lather. People tend to steer away from them. Yet, now and then, they win. I had an outstanding filly, Diamond Shower (Zephyr Zip–Jewel Flight) who would sweat up before just about every race. She was just a little slip of a thing, yet she won group races, including the AJC Sires' Produce, in which she knocked over the classy Bounding Away, and the $250,000 VRC Oaks, with Jim Cassidy sitting as quiet as a mouse, and ended up being voted Australian champion three year old of 1987. Before almost every one of her starts she would be in a lather of sweat. The only time she *didn't* break out was before the Thousand Guineas at Caulfield. That day she walked around the enclosure nice and calm and unruffled, then went out and ran the worst race of her career. Animals are so unpredictable. Just when you think you've got them worked out, they'll come out and do something *completely* different.

All the Diamond Shower story proves is that horses, in one respect at least, are like humans—each one of them is different. The thing I have admired most over the years about some of my really 'genuine' horses—like Colour Page and Tiger Town—is their sincerity. With horses like that there are no strings attached, no hidden agendas. How different that is from humans, who always seem to have an 'angle' in what they do—whether visible or invisible. A horse doesn't get inspiration from anywhere except within itself. Win, lose or draw on race day, it's still going to go home to a good feed of hay and a nice bed to lie on, as long as it's not in the minority of racehorses that don't get that treatment. No one will be yelling at it, or hitting it because of what it has or hasn't done. When a horse really puts in, it is from his or her own heart. And that is what I admire most about them—the fact that they haven't got an angle. They are just pure.

The true champions are made up of the right mix—the ability to be able to gallop better than most, backed by a constitution which can deliver, even under great difficulties. At this high level, people and horses meet on equal ground. Some people have constitutions that are such that no matter what is thrown at them, they can't be flattened. They just keep going. Deep down there is an indefinable quality within the brain which drives the body to the heights it reaches.

For (human) athletes and horses, the first two requirements of being a 'champion' are ability, and physical conformation. But while so many people have these things, they fall short on the third requirement—the inner strength to rise above the pack, rise above the difficulties that slow, or stop, everyone else, best described, I reckon, as the 'negative gremlins'.

The same rules apply to jockeys, of course, and I've had my moments with some of them over the years. I set high standards, and if they let me down, I was hard on them. I've had my blow-ups with jockeys, and some of them have made the press. One paper listed my 'numerous differences of opinion' with the likes of John Duggan, Rod Hardwick, Denis McClune, Grahame Horselman, Malcolm Johnston, Wayne Harris, Craig Nolan, Steve Schofield, Andrew Petith and Geoff Allendorf. There were probably others too. I remember *Sydney Morning Herald* journalist Bert Lillye being taken aback once when I told him I had 'stood down' Rod Hardwick for two weeks for not using the whip correctly. I was once described as being 'ruthless with jockeys who didn't ride to instructions'. It was true enough. I mellowed in later years, worked out there was a better way of doing things—and maybe the jocks and everybody around me are happy about that. I used to rant and rave at my staff, putting myself at a disadvantage. It was part of learning. You can't expect people to do it as well as you do—the fact is, they are only working for wages. For my own part, I was fanatically committed and focused on my goal of getting to the top in Sydney racing. There was even a highly publicised blow-up with Jim Cassidy, who I have long regarded as the best of the jockeys of my experience.

We brought Cassidy over from New Zealand after he had shot to prominence with that fabulous win on Kiwi in the Melbourne Cup of 1983. At Nebo Lodge he became the number one jockey for the Sangster–ARABS–S & M Fox triumvirate, and at least one newspaper had described the Mayfield-Smith–Cassidy partnership as the 'dominant force in Sydney racing' from 1985 to 1988. I have had a lot of top jockeys ride for me, and in ability, technique and skill, probably quite a few could be rated Cassidy's equal, but for me, he was, and is, the best. We have a close personal association and our wives, Maree and Helen, are very good friends, and maybe you could say that friendship clouds my view. But studied from any angle, Jim's record, the winning of the big races, the Group 1s, lifts him above the pack. He possesses that indefinable quality that I spoke of before, of being able to rise above adversity, of being able to produce on the big occasion.

Yet for a long time we were at arm's length. We had a significant falling-out, which I don't talk about much now. It is in the realms of history. The problem revolved around an unfortunate incident with a horse named Cruising at Rosehill, in June 1988. I am not going to rake over the details of what happened because I never have before, and there is nothing to be gained by it, but the horse's run precipitated a steward's enquiry, which resulted in Jim getting time. A full year out of the saddle. Rightly or wrongly, his tactics on the horse weren't to the stewards' satisfaction, and they outed him. From my point of view, I supported him as much as I could. The fact is, though, that when a jockey gets out there on the track, it is up to him what he does.

My view has always been that if a jockey makes an error of judgment, I can't be held responsible for it. After all, I have a vastly wider responsibility—to the people who employ me, and to the staff who are depending on me for a job.

Cassidy was distraught—and I understood that. It was twelve months out of his life, a mortal blow to a young jockey with such a potentially great career before him. We did not speak during the time of his suspension. The event caused a deep rift between us and we were effectively at arm's length for almost two and a half years. But time tends to heal such things if, deep down inside, there's a strong enough bond. By early 1991, any 'bad blood' that had existed between us was in the past and the media made a big fuss when we teamed up again, via Big Dreams in the Tod-man Slipper trial of March 1991. 'I'm really happy about us getting back as a team,' I told them. 'Some things occur in life which shouldn't—and this split with Jim was one of those things.' All is fine between Jim and me today, and when he rode Oliver Twist to win the Coongy Handicap for me in September 1999, I couldn't have been happier.

My philosophy of horse training hasn't changed too much over the years. I don't have some sort of preconceived idea in my head that I am a trainer of two year olds, or sprinters or stayers. I just take it horse by horse, with no preference. As I have said before, my racing education was strictly limited, and I have had to rely on persistence and an ability to assess each horse thoroughly and individually as they came along and work out, with gut feeling playing its part in that, what I reckoned was best for them.

That policy of taking horses as they come, with no pre-conceived idea about pigeonholing them as this or that, has probably had a lot to do with my success. Whether you're a human or a horse, there are two ways to get fit—eat well, and train hard. Essentially that sums up the broad view of what I have always done with my horses. I've kept it simple. And, you know, the further I move on in life, the more I realise that so many of the great things achieved are based on very *simple* foundations.

I had my main education with horses as a stockman. In that work, you knew that the horse was going to buck, and you *made* him buck—so you could get it out of him and prove to the animal that you could beat him. You virtually broke the horse's spirit, in a way, and that was the sort of mentality I grew up with. As a trainer I'd like to think my approach is a lot more sympathetic than that. I treat horses as individuals—I look at them and try to pick what they are feeling, or what their needs are at the time. After a while that becomes sort of second nature.

Horses are creatures of habit, adaptable to a pattern. And once they know the pattern, they are clever enough to avoid what's coming, if they have a mind to. If you break the pattern, change things, they are bamboozled for a while. Reverse psychology works well with horses. If you want a horse to go a particular way and he doesn't want to go that way, the trick is to try to make him believe you want him to go the other way. Probably then he'll go the way you want him to. With horses, a lot of things take time, time being *the* most important factor for humans in regard to horse management.

In today's 'instant' society, that presents more problems than perhaps it once did in the racing game when the world moved at a slower pace. The fundamental challenge for a trainer is to look after the horse in the long-term sense, but to look after the client too. Balancing that is sometimes not easy. If the horse is good enough, you don't want the owner to miss out on the big two-year-old prize money if you genuinely reckon the horse is capable of winning. But the main objective in training horses, as in any operation, must be to avoid wastage, to get that wastage percentage down. The best way to achieve that is to take time with your horses. If you get them up and racing too soon, put them under too much early pressure, then they're going to get arthritis and tendon injuries and chipped bones. Modern surgery might fix all that to the extent that they come back and win races but, once damaged, horses will never get to the potential they would have reached if they had remained perfectly sound.

It's a problem for our racing industry, the huge focus on the abundant prize money of the two-year-old season. The fact is that a horse's bones are not mature until five years of age, so high pressure racing at two years, with horses breaking one minute ten seconds for 1200 metres, is inevitably going to take its toll, physically *and* mentally. Many fall by the wayside. The ones that do get through represent a very small percentage, and generally they are the outstanding two year olds of their season, who run on natural ability, and do it fairly easily without stressing their bodies too much. A fact of Australian racing at present is that despite the arrival of the well-bred shuttle stallions in recent years—each of them servicing a book of mares *twice* the size of what it was a few years ago (100 mares, as against fifty)—the percentage of top-quality racehorses three years old and above has hardly increased. This raises a couple of questions: are the stallions being overworked? Do they only have a limited number of 'good shots' in them as far as siring quality horses goes?

There's no doubt that the depth and quality of both our older races and the weight for age programs are being affected by the obsession with the two year olds, and people wanting to capitalise quickly on the money they have invested.

It is a problem for the sport. Horses that would have

made good four or five year olds are gone. The two-year-old campaign has snuffed them out. The trend constitutes the nature and reality of modern racing, and it's a reflection of modern society. And it seems to be accelerating.

The obsession with young horses and quick returns here is so far removed from the patient and traditional ways of English horseracing. People here are often amazed when a stayer is brought out to Melbourne for the Cup with maybe only a handful of runs on the board even though the horse might be five or six. It's the way it is over there, and has been for countless years past; horses are given time to mature as the seasons unfold, one after the other. You'll see Derby winners with only three or four runs under their belt. There's a timeless quality about the English approach, which is very removed from the way we do things here.

Over the years the way of things in New Zealand has been different to our approach, too, with horses brought along more quietly—left out in the paddock rather than being stabled for example, and allowed to develop. But what is happening in New Zealand now is not good for racing there, or for Australasian racing as a whole, affecting the quest to maintain top-quality racehorses on our tracks in meaningful numbers. The emergence of big-money racing in Asia, allied with the reality of poor prize money in New Zealand, is leading to a trend of quality New Zealand horses disappearing 'up north'. The problem is, the only horses the Asian buyers are interested in are the good ones. The cream is being skimmed off the top. Good horses are being whisked out of the Australasian system. That's life in the modern era. You certainly can't blame owners for taking a good early return when they are confronted with big money offers.

In the training of horses, I certainly subscribe to the theory that you have to follow breeding lines to an extent.

There will always be exceptions to that rule, and contradictions. But you have to have *something* to follow at the start, and I have always been aware of breeding . . . at least until the horse comes out and virtually says to me, 'Look, I don't run the way my bloodlines suggest I should.' Then you adjust accordingly.

I suppose I know horses reasonably well after all these years, but I am no 'horse whisperer' and I envy that rare sort of people. I think it would be wonderful to be born with such deep natural intuition for the profession you have chosen. Sometimes I get a bit frustrated; I think to myself that I've been around horses all my life, yet I don't feel I understand them any more than I did years and years ago. I don't have a sense of 'getting inside their heads', or understanding how they really feel, any more than I ever did.

Then I read about someone like Monty Roberts, and read his own books, and I think how wonderful it would be to be blessed with that sort of gift. And he has a gift—no doubt about that. He wouldn't have survived this long if he didn't have something special. I always reckoned there were two things in life that could make an idiot of you—one of them is women, and the other is horses.

CHAPTER FIFTEEN

The Thrill of Africa

In 1987, my life changed. Forever. I had been in Sydney eleven years by then, working seven days a week. I had arrived at, and sustained for a second successive year, my goal of being the city's number one horse trainer, knocking over Tommy Smith again. That second win was important to me, even if it didn't quite give me the elation of the first. It was absolutely necessary to me to win it again to show that I was not a one-hit wonder. Along with the success came the bonus of more money than I had ever before even imagined in a modest life, providing the sort of comfort and financial security that I had never been within a bull's roar of up to that point. In 1987, wearied by hard years of struggling to get to the top, Maree and I decided we'd have a holiday—what was more, now we could afford one.

One morning Maree headed off to a city travel agent to see what was on offer. We wanted to go somewhere different, and Africa was our clear choice. As I mentioned earlier, that particular spark had been lit in me many years before. The distant memory of the elephant reaching so politely to take my proffered Mintie at the circus in Gordonvale had never left me. Neither had the thrill of seeing the movie *Hatari* for the first time. The call to go there, to see it for myself, was always within me, deep down inside. On TV we had watched documentaries on the growing problems of the wildlife in Africa, of species that were threatened because of the actions of man. We had seen programs on the horrifying damage being done by poaching, and how it had become a massive problem. That had stirred concern in us too, encouraged us further to go and see for ourselves.

Now, the chance was here. Back then, not too many Aussies were heading that way on their holidays. It's only over the last ten years or so that the African safari thing has really taken off. On that first trip, thirteen years ago, we flew to Johannesburg, then on to Botswana and Zimbabwe, and the Victoria Falls. Africa turned out to be everything we had expected it to be. This is living, I thought, as I took it all in . . .

The first real surge of excitement and wonder for me came after we had taken an Air Botswana flight to Maun, which in those days was just a dusty little shantytown on the edge of the delta. Today, the town has grown so much it's just about unbelievable. Safely through customs there, we transferred to a Cessna and headed onwards, towards the Moremi Game Reserve on the edge of the Okavango Delta. On the short-hop trips over there the pilots don't bother taking the planes up too far, and I suppose we were at no more than about 240 metres when we spotted a big herd of elephants, spooked by the plane and moving with urgency through the trees below. For a boy from North Queensland whose only contact with elephants had been via the occasional passing circus long ago, and through TV documentaries—this was something.

It was an eye-opening trip, a wonderful first taste of the country that was to progressively burrow its way into my life, and into Maree's. From the Okavango Delta we flew north to a place called Allan's Camp near the Savuti Channel, then on to the Chobe Game Lodge, on the Chobe River. We finished in some comfort, staying at the Victoria Falls Hotel, where the roar of the falls provided the background music. We saw many magnificent animals, especially in the Savuti, where the lions and elephants roamed.

The whole experience left a deep and lasting impression on me. The essence of going to Africa is that you know you have experienced something of value. When I went there and saw how beautiful the country was, and how truly wonderful the animals, my thought was, they can't just let this die.

From that very first trip (of ten so far) I felt I began to change as a person. Each subsequent trip has added a layer to that—of calmness, of a sense of what is real and what is not in the lives we lead. Africa represented a whole new world, requiring a different way of thinking. I have always searched for something outside the mundane routine of life, and probably more so once I was locked into the discipline, dictated by necessity, of being a horse trainer. Learning to fly a helicopter was one way I tackled it. I like flying, although I confess that sometimes it scares me—yet it was a challenge, a breaking away. It was my attempt, back then, to get my mind into a different thought process, because horse training becomes all-consuming—it goes on seven days a week, year after year; the trap is that it can become all you speak about, or think about. Instead of expanding, your mind narrows to a very specific involvement.

I'm a bloke with plenty of commonsense, I reckon, although I have never regarded myself as being a smart person academically. Even though I have spent my life searching for answers, reading a lot, I suppose the feeling has always been in me that I was never going to rise to any great intellectual level. But I have kept searching—and will keep searching. Africa, from the beginning, changed my thinking, as if a switch had been turned. Experiencing that provided a great release from the mindset that had been my reality before I went there.

Africa has a smell about it, a smell of the bush. At places like Nairobi and Johannesburg, the diesel fumes drown it out, but at other, quieter, places, you can step off the plane and know instantly you are 'back'. There are a lot of fires in Africa, and it is quite a vivid experience to be hit by the smell of burning wood and bush that is so distinctive—somehow so *African*.

For me, Africa has provided the sort of inspiration that I believe we all desperately need—however we get it—in our lives. I talk a lot about animals, and my serious concern about how species are threatened by the way we humans conduct ourselves. In no way does that take away from the importance of our own species. If you do something really well and inspire other people to carry it on or do better, then I believe you have contributed to the evolution of our own species. There are heaps of people out there who have done great things, and we have all been inspired by them. I think the younger generations need to be made aware that great achievements in life are often accomplished by ordinary people—doing the extraordinary. You can move a lot of people in the right directions in their lives just by doing those things in life that are important, and by doing them well. I strongly believe that having compassion for other people, for other species and for the environment is a responsibility that belongs to us all. I reckon it's important that each of us at least *tries* to leave something good behind in life.

True heroes to me are people like World War II's 'Weary' Dunlop, with his ability to rise above misery and suffering to inspire those around him, and Nelson Mandela, surely one of the greatest figures of the century. To contemplate what he managed to do in South Africa is to be inspired. For him to have been locked up for twenty-six years, yet to somehow through that time retain both his ideals and his sanity, then come out and turn around an entire country . . . Mandela truly is a 'hero', a word bandied around rather too freely for my liking, and especially on the sporting field. For me the first qualification of a hero is that they've achieved something extraordinary, something of value—against the odds.

Mandela's strength, of body and mind, should be an inspiration to us all. He refused to allow the system to brutalise him, to reduce him to the lowest common denominator of prison life. For all those long years he was able to rise above that—then, eventually, to confront what had been an inflexible apartheid regime, and inspire the change that the rest of the world was calling for.

The most admirable thing about him is that, unlike most people in his position of power throughout history, he genuinely possesses the qualities of humility and forgiveness, and a great sense of 'community', which enabled him to bring people together, largely avoiding the violence, the killing, the civil war that could so easily have eventuated. Many in his position would have come out of prison bent on revenge for the injustices they had been handed. But Mandela had the grace and the greatness to rise above it, and to immediately focus on the bigger task at hand.

He was the sort of leader that every country hopes for, but few get. Regrettably, our own leaders in Australian government fall a long way short of the Mandela model. To me, so many of them are in it for themselves, making up a big Boys Club, interested mainly in themselves, their party and preserving power with the good of the country a poor fourth. We should continue to hope for better leadership—someone like Mandela, whose messages of inspiration surely permeated all the way down to the young.

To some extent I feel sorry for young people today. For them, it undoubtedly seems that things in our world don't look as good as they once did. The talk is of world pollution, of disappearing species, of overcrowding and worrying climate change. All of that must weigh on the generations which will carry us into the future. Probably more than any other group, they are in need of inspiration; they need to understand that, no matter how hopeless things look, if you adopt a positive and *persistent* attitude in pursuing your ideals and dreams, then things can come out very well; that once you give up, that is the finish of it, but that *nothing* is finished with you personally until you make the decision to give up; that even though you might be *getting* a beating, you are not beaten until you give up.

Sitting around a campfire in Africa, with time moving slowly, gives you a chance to think about things that rarely come to the surface in the busy lives we lead in big cities. I came back from that first trip in 1987 with my beliefs that there is nothing more beautiful in life than the natural environment, the natural world, reinforced. As far as I am concerned, this is the purest form of beauty available to us.

Nature can be represented as a tapestry at this point in history, when people now happen to briefly hold the stage. We humans are just a single thread in that tapestry, and while we persist in breaking every other thread in it, we face the danger of being left alone . . . the only thread left, flapping in the breeze. At that point we'll wither on the vine, and be dead. In essence, in destroying the other threads, we are destroying ourselves as a species. These are no great, profound thoughts. They are just commonsense. And if this book can encourage people to think about some of these things—and act—then it will have fulfilled the purpose I had hoped it would have.

I admit to despairing of it all in my darker moments. To consider such pastimes as cock-fighting or bull-fighting—or anything else in which 'pleasure' is provided to humans by the spectacle of an animal dying—is to think inevitably of the dark, evil recesses that exist within humankind. So, too, in our treatment of each other at times. We slaughter each other endlessly, through murder and war—so what chance is there for the animals?

And it happens, generation after generation, and no matter how much it is publicised and condemned, or what punishment is handed out for acts of man's inhumanity to man, it still keeps happening. You would have thought that through the gradual evolution of our species we might have left all that behind. We talk about how great and superior we are, and how we have a certain spirit that puts us above any other species. Sometimes I think we're just kidding ourselves.

There is a saying, 'There are enough resources in the world for people's needs, but not enough for people's greed'. It's so true. It is the 1 per cent of people who, through their greed, deny the other 99 per cent and affect the chances of future generations—they are the problem.

To me the danger is this: that future generations may inherit a world that is no more than a 'desert'. Spiritually, or from the point of view of the soul, what's the use of being alive if you can't relate to something else that is natural and beautiful in the world? Everything man makes these days has got to be switched on and plugged in. Switch it off, unplug it and it's useless. Meanwhile, the natural things fade away, or are destroyed. We won't survive just on the technology and the false 'nature' we've built around inanimate things. Meanwhile, people go crazy in the urban environment in which they're trapped.

So, what are we as individuals to do about it? Well, *something* in my view. Okay, it might be seen as pushing shit uphill, or pissing into the wind, but we can't just shrug our shoulders, stand back and say, 'This is hopeless, so why worry about it?' And that's what a lot of people do, virtually throwing the problem to others, to the next generation. 'Let them worry about it . . . let them deal with it.' Such an attitude is inward-looking, destructive and totally selfish.

There are many species in our world long gone already, and others disappearing or seriously threatened. I am heartened only by the groundswell of awareness and care that seems to have emerged in the community in these last fifteen years or so. The healing process has begun, but whether it can rise above the destructive forces which are already in place—that's the question. Is it too late?

In my early days in North Queensland there was never a thought that things would change. Australia, after all, was a place of so much space and seeming abundance; there was plenty of everything, and always would be. As a kid I used to think about the world quite a bit, and I decided that the oceans and the forests were *so* vast that man wouldn't even be able to penetrate them; it never even occurred to me that he might one day *destroy* them. That's the way it was back then. People thought nothing would ever run out: we'd never cut down all the jungles or forests; lakes would never be fished out; animals would never be slaughtered to the point that they disappeared. After all, there was so much of everything . . .

Well, thirty-five or forty years on, the fact is we're hammering hell out of the planet, and if the brakes aren't put on in the very near future, the whole thing will be turned into a swamp-hole, devoid of life—a bloody desert blowing away with every passing wind, upon which nothing can survive. Including us.

In Africa, most of the damage done to the animal population was done in the nineteenth century, when there was mass slaughter of just about every single species. For 'sport'. The killing and poaching of today is nowhere near what it was back then. And in fact when the healing process began in Africa early in the twentieth century, it was the big game hunters who kicked it off. The wisest of them turned conservationist—or at least to 'selective' hunting—to preserve what they could see by then was being lost. That beginning has been progressively built on by the work of the National Parks and Reserves movement. The emphasis now is on extending national reserves to create more habitat, given that the loss of habitat represents the biggest danger of all to the animals. Loss of habitat leads to an inevitable reduction in prey density, and increasingly the maintenance of prey density is being recognised as the most important element in habitat protection.

In Peter Matthiessen's book *Tigers in the Snow*, he presents a sobering statistical view of what has happened to the world's tigers, figures that typify the problem across the board. At the beginning of the last century, 100,000 tigers still survived around the world. Three of the geographic populations, and perhaps even four, have been extinguished in Matthiessen's lifetime, and he believes at least three others may vanish forever in the first decade of the twenty-first century. He gives present estimates of tiger numbers in the wild as ranging between 4600 and 7700.

The commitment of some people in the long, ongoing fight has been beyond measurement. Almost certainly there'd be no rhino left for the world to marvel at if it hadn't been for the changing attitude of the early 1900s, and the efforts of a lot of special people then, and in the years since. Most of the world turned its back: this, after all, was *Africa*'s problem. But thankfully—even when the white rhino were reduced at the turn of the century to about ten in number—there were people in South Africa who fought on, eventually breeding them all the way back from that fragile moment to the point where they are now off the endangered list. Nowadays, people go to Africa specially to see the rhino, which are only there because enough people thought them worth fighting for. That sort of battle fought over the rhino is what gives life meaning as far as I am concerned. The story is repeated over and over, as with the whales, once hunted to the edge of extinction but now the centre of a new global money-making industry: whale watching.

My deep concern for animals, and about what we are doing to them, certainly includes Australia too. We have lost far too many species here, and I am ashamed of our record. During the short period of white settlement we have destroyed *so many* species that, very likely, pound for pound, we're the worst in the world . . .

I thought about all these things on that first trip in 1987, and I have thought about them ever since. As my concern for the animals and the natural things grew, doing something significant in that area—rather than in my own career—became the most important thing in my life. Increasingly as the years went by, my career became a means to an end, rather than the other way around. My belief is this: that animals are very important to human existence. You only have to see how we humans react to dogs and cats and other animals. People need animals. The dying-out of species, therefore, is a tragedy—not just for the animals involved, but for the human race as well. And there's not too much time left. There is plenty that can be saved, and time enough, but not if we just let everything drift to the edge for another twenty years or so.

I don't believe the human race can exist by itself, with nothing else natural to complement it. The spirits and souls of all of us would wither up and die if all we had left was to gaze into computer screens, or to prop ourselves up with the latest technology. We *owe* nothing less to the people coming behind us than to give them the same opportunities that we have to interact with the things of nature. To allow the natural things to be destroyed, to allow species to be wiped out, represents a shocking neglect of our responsibilities as human beings. It is that realisation and ideal that have driven me since I first went to Africa. In our small way Maree and I have tried to help ever since. And we will keep doing so.

I feel now as I did when I returned from that first trip. Trying to get it all into words back then, I told journalist John Burney in August 1987:

> What gets me is the way we are just changing everything, upsetting the earth until it's completely buggered. In India the tiger population has been eroded by the human population to the point that the only place you'll see them soon is in the bloody zoo. It's the same with the whales. The rhinos in Africa are down to about 5000—and why? Because they want to make dagger handles from the horns or grind them down for aphrodisiacs when anybody with any brains knows you might as well take a Bex powder. Look at the pollution spewing into the air. Too many people are taking the view of short-term monetary gain rather than looking at the whole structure and considering what it will be like in 100 years. It is just terrible to see beautiful things being destroyed. What about the kids who are coming up behind us? What kind of world are we leaving them? Surely to God we owe them something!

Although heartened by some of the things that have happened in the thirteen years since, my sentiments remain essentially the same. And I will continue to ask the questions.

That first trip planted a seed—and in what was obviously fertile soil. When we left Africa to fly home, there was no conscious acceptance that inevitably we would be back one day. That is something that grows steadily within you—and for me, it did. The place changes you. I think it makes you more tolerant. It certainly makes you more aware of what the world really is today, rather than clinging to some idea of keeping it the way it was fifty years ago. The opportunity that the trip provided to interact with beautiful and natural things left a deep impression on me. I recognised I had experienced something of value in my life. I felt I had been dragged out of the ordinary life to which all of us to varying degrees are attached and had experienced something unique, something to be treasured. Probably without quite realising it, we came back to Australia as different people.

Africa does that to you.

CHAPTER SIXTEEN

The Place That Lives in My Heart

The first trip we took to Africa in 1987 was followed by another, and then another . . . ten times so far for me, and nine for Maree. The sights and sounds and smells of Africa are in my mind, in my blood . . . in my heart. Many of our memories are captured in our scrapbooks, on film, and in the diary we kept of our 1995 trek. Other memories live on only in our minds. Sometimes they are memories on a grand scale, sometimes tiny—the fleeting glimpse of an animal framed by the setting sun. In this chapter, I will do my best to share some of those memories with you, fragments of what it has meant to us to have tasted the 'African experience' . . .

With Maree I am in a flimsy reed hut with an A-frame roof in Savuti Elephant Camp, on our second trip there. The drought at that time in Botswana was deep and long, and around the camp there had been placed an electric 'hot' wire, powered by a battery and designed to keep the elephants out.

In times of drought elephants have been known to come into camps to try to break open the water pipes. A single live wire generally does the job of keeping them at bay.

At some time in the early hours we are woken by a strange noise. Maree describes it later as like the sound of wind funnelling along a reed pipe. Through the tent's thin gauze window is an astonishing sight. A huge bull elephant is on the other side of the wire, reaching far across with his trunk to pick at the grass growing around our tent. The noise we hear is his breath through the trunk as he leans delicately across the wire. He is almost within touching distance—a massive, magnificent animal. Making the scene even more dramatic is the fact that he is framed by the light of a brilliant full moon over his shoulder. We stand there silently, hearts pounding—our emotions a mix of wonder, apprehension and enjoyment . . .

⁂

We crossed the Mara River one morning and drove down through Kenya to the border of Tanzania at the time the annual wildebeest migration was on. The ground falls away into Tanzania and we could see for miles across the rolling hills, and all of it was covered with animals—by wildebeest, and by the zebra which travel with them. It was just amazing to be driving through the middle of that, to be surrounded by hundreds of thousands of animals on the move. As they ran by, the animals would glance at us with no more than indifference and keep going. The columns stretched as far as the eye could see, all the way to the horizon, the wildebeest and zebra looking like ants in the distance. It was one of those moments in life that we all occasionally encounter, when we're literally stopped in our tracks by the beauty of something or the size of something.

It was inspiring. It was also something that happens a fair bit when you travel in Africa—you tend to get overwhelmed by things. The sheer size of the population and the realisation that 90 per cent of that population is living in absolute poverty certainly have that sort of overwhelming effect.

The zebra and wildebeest move together, in a huge annual circuit which takes them from the Serengeti, following the rains and the grass up into the Masai Mara, then back down again into Tanzania and into the Serengeti. It is a cycle that has continued for years. Wildebeest are regarded as rather silly animals, but the fact is that they are great survivors. Fossil remains have been found from two million years ago. Predators follow the yearly migration, the lions at the top of the pecking order.

Maree and I did our best to capture on film the immensity of what we saw. We failed. Photos and video film just can't reflect the huge sweep of what unfolds when the animals are on the move. But the scene, at least, lives on in our minds . . .

* * *

One of Africa's most awe-inspiring experiences is a first glimpse of the Ngorogoro Crater in Tanzania. The road there winds up through the bush with no hint of what lies beyond. Then, suddenly, there's a gap in the trees, and in front of you lies this amazing place, a vast natural bowl. Once, eons ago, it was a volcano; now it's just bush, filled with huge numbers of animals. The first time I saw it, the enormity of the place—what it was and what it is—hit me with a force so strong it felt physical. It was a revelation. All the country around that part of Africa and through to Kenya is volcanic. Kilimanjaro is a volcano. Mt Kenya, its cone washed away millions of years ago, is an extinct volcano, its jagged peaks composed of solidified magma which plugged the original cone.

My first encounter with the Sesriem Dunes of the Namibian Desert stays strongly in my mind's eye too. These are the world's highest and biggest dunes, stretching for sixty kilometres. The road that runs through the middle of them is a dry river bed, almost always passable considering that the river flows only every twenty years or so. The dunes change colour as the day goes on, from pink, to peach, to red, to brown. They are amazing—so strange they seem to be unreal . . .

* * *

A first flight across the Okavango Delta in Botswana, most of which is desert or semi-desert, is something never forgotten. The country in the Okavango is largely wetlands, with higher, drier areas scattered between, on which stand tall palm trees. At 15,000 square kilometres the Okavango is the largest inland delta in the world, a truly wonderful place in the west–northwest of a peaceful and prosperous (for Africa) country as big as France. And the experience never pales. On a flight across the Delta on our latest trip (in 1999) we swooped low over a group of elephants, about eight of them, making their way out of the water and up towards a clump of palm trees. One old bull lifted his head up towards the plane and you could hear his trumpet over the sound of the engine. It was a beautiful and remarkable sight and sound.

The pilots who fly the Delta are real bush jockeys. They don't in the least mind hedge-hopping, and often you'll find yourself only a hundred feet or so above the ground. The Delta is home to a wonderful array of animals, including big mobs of hippo which you can visit in a more up-close way via *makoros*—small, fairly fragile dugout canoes, traditionally made from the jackalberry tree, but today more often from fibreglass—which glide through the papyrus channels. A trip aboard a *makoro* carries with it some element of danger—the chance that you will suddenly come upon a hippo in a narrow stretch of water. Statistics show that hippos kill more people in Africa annually than any other animal, but the fact is, the number of people who get hurt or killed is pretty minimal when you consider the numbers who expose themselves to that environment, and to the animals in it. The delta has so much to offer, with its elephants, hippos, crocodiles and more than 400 species of birds. Dusk on the Okavango is magic.

⁂

It's not just the animals that can surprise you in Africa. On our long trek (in 1995) we were surprised by the numbers of people who would just appear out of the bush, far from any town or 'civilisation'. Driving back from West Uganda we took a short cut down a dirt road flanked by thick jungle. Here and there along this seemingly remote road, people would suddenly appear out of nowhere, ghosting out of the thick foliage. Elsewhere, people would be waiting by the side of the road, untroubled, as we discovered, if it took them a couple of days to pick up the lift that might take them to some distant town. Time moves to a different beat over there . . .

Heading across the Namibian Desert one day, en route to a place called Walvis Bay—a fine deep-water port, the best on the west African coast and once a big South African naval town and depot—we saw a tiny figure far off, shimmering in the heat haze. At first we thought it must have been an ostrich, but then as we drew closer it became apparent that it was a bloke on a pushbike heading back the way we had come, loaded up with bags and what seemed to be his worldly possessions. It was late afternoon, and there was no chance he would reach any sort of town that night. It gave us pause for thought; we thought *we* were adventurous as we drove around Africa in our air-conditioned four-wheel drive. And here was a bloke on a pushbike, travelling on his own and crossing the bloody Namibian Desert at night! We found out later that he was on a ride for charity, having already pushbiked his way around India and Asia.

***

Close encounters with some of Africa's animal inhabitants have been a fact of life on our trips. We've had a couple of brushes with elephants that could have turned out differently. Once I was with our mate in Kenya, Marcus Russell, on Segera Ranch in the Laikipia district. Marcus, son of a father who was one of Africa's 'white hunters', has been involved in wildlife conservation and tourism over the years. He is very passionate about the conservation of animals, and very knowledgable about the subject. Most of our early 'education' on Africa came from him. We had gone one afternoon to an outlying hut on the property where a bull elephant had been causing problems for the bloke who lived there, a worker who looked after the cattle. Worried for his family, the man had asked Marcus to come up and chase the elephant away.

When we arrived, there were two bull elephants standing not far from the hut and, as we approached them (on foot), one of them turned and started to head towards us. I wasn't too concerned at that stage, but when Marcus started to backtrack and pick up speed, and then fired off a shot, I thought, jeeze, I'd better get going—he knows more about this sort of situation than I do! The bull had his head down and the trunk curled and was on the charge, but the sound of the shot checked him rightly enough and, showing surprising speed, we made it back to the four-wheel drive.

Maree had the bruises to prove it after another, similar encounter. She was filming from the back of the truck on Segera Ranch and we had stopped near some females and babies. One old matriarch took exception to our presence and charged the truck. 'We'd better get out of here—quick,' said Marcus, and gunned the accelerator. With that, Maree went flying in the back. Her eye to the camera, she had not realised how close the elephant was. In fact it was right at the door when we took off, its trunk almost reaching into the truck.

If we had been killed or injured in those sorts of situations, it would have been our own fault—because we had gone over the line, pressured the animal to the extent that it reacted the way it did. It happens a lot in Africa, and it's often how people get hurt. You get this sort of adrenalin rush and you push your luck a bit, do things that are not really sensible in the light of day. We have not been blameless in that regard. The more time you spend there, the more you understand the animals—and the more respect you have for them. You learn to give them space.

We have had our brushes with smaller African inhabitants too—with snakes and scorpions. Heading out to go to the toilet one day in a camp in Zimbabwe, I heard a hissing noise. I looked down and there was a snake—and by that time in our travels I had learned that the ones that hissed were the most dangerous! Maree sort of got involved in this—in the worst possible way. I called for her to come over and have a look, but to keep her distance. Meanwhile a couple of Africans had joined in too, and they were laughing at the fact the snake was there. Unimpressed by the attention, the snake took off from the drain where he had been lying—unfortunately choosing an escape route which took him directly towards Maree. Her high jump was good enough for the Olympics.

Camped in Northern Kenya one night in 1995, I was out with a torch checking the Land Rover and the tent before we went to bed. I was wearing a pair of scuff shoes, open at the top. Near our unrolled swag in the tent I saw what I thought was a leaf blowing across the ground. Fortunately I had a closer look, which revealed that it was, in fact, a large scorpion. To have had one of those in the bed would not have been a good idea. They are dangerous things; one of Richard Leakey's daughters died from a scorpion bite, the time it took to get her from northern Kenya to treatment in Nairobi being the problem. That's a reality of Africa, and of the Australian bush too: if you get bitten by something particularly poisonous and happen to be a long way from help, then inevitably you're in trouble.

When you're in a camp in Africa, leaving the tent to go to the toilet at night can be quite an adventure, as you would have gathered from my snake encounter. The first thing you tend to do is to shine the torch around, and identify the different eye colours and shapes of any animals nearby. Then it's 'eyes . . . okay, antelopes'—or whatever it happens to be.

Once at a bush camp I had a dose of the runs on an evening when lions were calling very close by. I was in quite a dilemma. Lion or no lion, I'm not going to shit myself, I thought. So out I went, for a very uncomfortable few minutes, shining the torch around me throughout the operation. Fortunately, the only cat I encountered was a genet cat, small and spotted, with a long body, his eyes sparkling in the beam of the torch. I guess it says something about my personal hygiene—and perhaps about civilised man—that I would rather confront a lion than accept the (certain) alternative of that night. The roar of a lion close by at night makes every fibre of your body tingle and vibrate. I was dreaming in our tent in a camp one night when a lion roar pushed its way into the dream. My mind told me there was no lion in the dream and I woke with a start just as a male lion roared again—very, very close by. It's an incredible sound which produces an equal mixture of fear and excitement. The African bush is alive with sound at night: the rasping call of the lions and, sometimes, their full bloodcurdling roar; the 'conversation' of elephants; the whooping, cackling call of the hyenas . . . and all the others, that marvellous mix of large and small and the extraordinary.

❋❋❋

We have seen a heartening improvement, in both attitude and action, with animal poaching in the thirteen years or so that we have been going to Africa. But it remains a terrible problem in central and western Africa, where countless baboons, gorillas, monkeys and many other animals are being slaughtered for bush meat—an inevitable reality of life in a country so short of food. Many people still look on the parks as being full of meat. The opening up of inaccessible parts of Africa—the building of roads to cut deep into timbered country—adds to the problem, virtually creating highways for poachers into areas where animals were once protected because of the sheer impenetrability of them.

The poaching of elephants for ivory, and rhino for their horns, has lessened, an improvement brought about by the actions of people within Africa, by world awareness, and by such things as ivory bans. More and more young Africans are being exposed at a very young age to the problems that exist for their country in diminishing animal numbers.

With awareness and education comes pride, and a growing determination to protect the animals that are there. In South Africa more and more reserves are opening all the time. Mining land is being converted back, and ranches and cattle properties are becoming reserves following the reintroduction of wildlife.

Maree and I have seen first-hand the brutal results of poaching raids: slaughtered elephants, their tusks hacked off. And we have seen more than that. Before we left Australia in 1995, I recalled in a newspaper interview a terrible experience from our second visit to Africa, at a time when elephants were stalked in their thousands, the ivory ripped from their bodies. My memory was this:

> We were in Tsavo East National Park, a very big park, and we saw elephants that had been slaughtered indiscriminately by AK47s. They mowed down babies and everything. It wasn't just one clean-kill shot either. Somalis would come up and ambush them as a group and knock over whatever they could. You can imagine the distress and the injuries. They were even chopping the ivory out of the elephants' heads before they were dead—killing babies to get a piece of ivory less than six inches long.

As Maree observed at the time, to see an elephant that has been poached, lying in the dirt with its face cut off, is a deeply saddening sight.

✖✖✖

The whole thing is so difficult. It's all very well for us as educated people to sit back here in some faraway country, expounding on what should be done. But to try to convey that widely to people in some corner of Africa, to uneducated people with no real concern for the animals, people who just see them as pests or as a means of making money, because that is the way they have been brought up—it's not easy. Although you feel that the animals are the victims, because the threat is presented by humans, you also have to sympathise with the plight of the people as you drive around and realise how little most of them have, how desperate things are . . . how hopeless life must look to them. They are brought into the world, and somehow they have to survive. It is hard to get through to them that animals which might be causing them problems need to be saved for the greater good of the country. What is happening now—which is very good—is that the people are being directly involved in conservation projects through which funds come back to them, and benefit them as a community.

On any visit, the plight of the African people in many places—some African countries are far better off than others—is a cause of great and ongoing frustration. You want to help, but how can you? How can you say to one, 'I'll help you,' then to the next, 'No, I can't help you.' The only way you can do something for someone special is in the background, away from all the others. You feel helpless.

The people really to blame are those who have perpetrated the trade in animal products, and those who—innocently or ignorantly—buy ivory and rhino horn without realising the suffering and cruelty involved in getting it.

The truth of it is this: no-one will go to Africa once the animals are gone. The continent is, after all, unique—the only place in the world where you can go to see such an incredible variety of animals. Without them, Africa would be finished—the people wouldn't come, and the foreign exchange would no longer be flowing into the country.

But things are getting better—that's the good news—and especially so as the great and true idea takes hold that Africa must have its animals, must care for its animals, if it is not to become some unvisited dustbowl of the future, a hopeless morass of humanity with people reverting back to being like rats in the gutter, just trying to survive. The magnificent animals provide hope for the country, for they are the reason why people visit Africa, bringing with them the money that the country desperately needs. The people will suffer even more than now if the tourists stop going there. The long-term insurance for the animals is that people from richer countries go there to see them, giving Africa the lifeblood of foreign currency.

So the best way people can support the wildlife, the natural things—of Africa, of Australia or wherever—is to travel there as tourists. By doing that we give the people fighting to preserve the great and natural things of our world the chance to pay for that fight, to defend what they are doing when others in the population demand, 'What about us?'

The great paradox of Africa is that we humans are the predators, the killers of animals, but we are the only ones who can save them too. It's to be hoped that the small percentage of people who have the heart to fight to preserve the wonderful natural things we have in this world grows and grows as the years go by. Too many people have the attitude, 'Well, it doesn't concern *me*,' or 'It's too hard—what can *I* do?' Sadly, there are still idiots today who go out and kill animals for sport. It still amazes me that people can think they're something special when they pose over the carcass of an animal they have killed with high-powered rifles from a long distance, ensuring their own safety. To me, they are just fools. A real hunter tracks and gets up close to his prey on the ground, taking a risk and giving the animal a chance to fight back. To me, any other way is 'insipid assassination'.

Chapter Seventeen

Breaking Free

By 1995, I had been in Sydney for nineteen years. I had won three successive trainers' premierships before T.J. Smith reclaimed the title in 1988–89, and been close in others. It had been ten years since I'd arrived at what had seemed my 'impossible dream'—to make the long trek from my tiny caravan in Cairns and become Sydney's top horse trainer. Increasingly as the early 1990s unfolded, I felt as though I was on a treadmill, or caught in a revolving door. Nearing forty-eight years of age, I sensed that mentally I was going nowhere. Finally, it reached the point where I knew I had to break free. Before I tell you about the step that Maree and I took, I'll tell you the 'why' of it.

I had continued to train with pretty solid success into the 1990s, although on a cut-down scale from the start of that decade. Back on 1 March 1991, the Nebo Lodge operation—which had given me the platform for the premiership successes of 1985–86, 1986–87 and 1987–88—

had ceased to be. In November 1990, Bob Lapointe explained the decision to close the stable: 'Our decision to wind up the Nebo Lodge business was prompted by the value and redevelopment potential. Training racehorses at Nebo Lodge is not making the best use of this valuable site.' (The place where Nebo Lodge stood is now a shopping centre.) Robert Sangster had been slowly reducing his thoroughbred stock throughout the world over the previous couple of years. By then (in 1990) we had about sixty horses in work; two years earlier it had been 100.

From 1991, temporarily at the same premises (renamed Marauding Lodge Stables), then at Kensington Parade, Randwick, I headed back into public training, after thirteen years as a predominantly private trainer, without the umbrella of the syndicate, but still with clients such as Bob Lapointe, Robert Sangster and Fox Investments on the books. The colt Big Dreams was the star of the stable back then.

The loss of the premiership title to Smith back in 1988–89 had not been unexpected. A journalist at the time wrote of 'the raucous clamour of [my] two rivals [Smith and Bart Cummings] bidding ever higher on yet another perfectly bred yearling with yet another "potential champion" tag on it.' The pair of them had spent and spent at yearling sales throughout Australasia over the previous two years. In an interview in April 1989, with the certainty now there that I wouldn't win for a fourth straight year (standings then were: Smith seventy-two winners, Cummings fifty-five, Mayfield-Smith forty-six and a half), I said:

> I wouldn't say it's upset me [losing the title], you could just say that I'm basically not content with being anything less than No 1 after being No 1 for three years. I came from nothing and I came from the backwoods of Australia, so to speak.

I've crossed more dry gullies than anyone else to get to where I have. I mean, the odds of getting from where I was to where I have would have been about a billion to one. I'm the kind of person who realises that things fluctuate, fortunes fluctuate, in life—and more so in racing.

I reflected ruefully at the time, 'I might go to the sales and spend a couple of million, but then you have Tommy Smith and Bart Cummings spending six or seven million and buying all the top yearlings.'

Into the 1990s my team was leaner in numbers, and without the critical mass needed to be a premiership contender. I knew that a trainer needed seventy to eighty horses in full training to really prosper in Sydney racing, but with a financial squeeze gripping the land, I took the sensible step of cutting back after the Nebo Lodge era came to an end, figuring that in a downturn it was better to be smaller than bigger. The daily and weekly routines, however, continued unabated—the early mornings, the countless phone calls, the pressure, the race days, the sense of being trapped. I reached the point where I knew it had to change . . .

At about the time that Maree and I became involved in the black rhino program at Western Plains Zoo, Dubbo—something that became increasingly important to us both—I arrived at the stage where I knew that to carry on being a race trainer—winning some races, making some money—no longer gave life meaning for me. And I believe anyone's life has got to have meaning and purpose—and I mean *decent* meaning and *decent* purpose. I have always been the sort of person who—apart from liking the bush, the animals, the natural things of this world—likes to make life interesting. And what makes life interesting is variety: exploring, absorbing new things, new experiences, different cultures. I felt back in 1995 a deep need to do something more meaningful, to make some sort of mark. I wasn't looking for recognition in that, I just wanted to make some sort of significant contribution.

Two things that have always been most important to me in my life have been my independence and my ability to move on. To me these characteristics are at the heart of what life is about, giving us the ability to break the chains of the same old bloody humdrum things. We all go through similar daily processes, forcing ourselves to go forward, convincing ourselves how good things are, when in reality very often we're just plonking along, with nothing to lift us above the daily grind.

In 1995, I looked around me and saw people trapped in racing. I saw it in their faces and in their behaviour—so predictable, because it had to be that way. I understood. I was there myself. And life's like that: it will trap you within narrow parameters if you let it.

I felt back then as I feel now, that I didn't want to be tied down, that life was too short to lock myself away. But when you have a 'reputation' as being good at something, it makes it even harder to break away. You inevitably think, I've got a good reputation—if I leave this, I'll never get back. But the big question is this: if that reputation is going to make your life ordinary and mundane, then what is the good of it?

In modern society with its soft comforts a lot of people have lost any sense of challenge and adventure. Being tied down by commitments, by kids, by personal circumstances, they see no alternative to the lives they lead, and very often they are simply not game to break away. But sometimes you've just got to say: 'Look, this is my life—I'm only going to get one shot at it. I'm going to do it!'

I think that very often we make out that what we're doing is a hell of a lot more important than it really is.

When we're in some job or profession we think, I can't possibly leave this, because they can't do without me. Well, they'll do without you okay if you happen to drop dead. Life will go on. The fact is that we're not that important. None of us. We're all just human beings, just 'passing through'.

I have learned this in my fifty-three years: that if you want to make life interesting, you've got to go out and do things and take a chance. Tomorrow is promised to no-one, so why worry about tomorrow? Sure, you've got to plan for it to an extent so you keep going, but you can't let it worry you to the point that you're not game to break away. Confronting difficult, different things is part of what we should do. If you get through when you do that, it gives you a great sense of achievement—and if you don't, hopefully you'll learn something along the way which makes you a better person anyway, a person of strong character, a more interesting person with more to contribute to the business of living this gift . . . life.

It was in line with all these shared beliefs about life that Maree and I made the decision that we would give up training, leave racing and go back to Africa. Permanently. By 1995, we had been to Africa eight times, and it held a deep-down place in both our hearts. This was a weighty decision, made slowly and steadily, but one we were certain about once we arrived at it. I can reveal now that we made up our minds twelve months before the news became public, having decided at the Brisbane Winter Carnival of 1994 that it was what we wanted to do—and would do.

We started making plans quietly, without telling a soul and without changing anything too dramatically, too quickly or too noticeably. It was a secret well kept—to the extent that, until the day I gave notice at the stable, a month out from our departure date, no-one had caught on. To that point I had shared the news only with Mrs Fox, out of my respect for her. She had understood, and not breathed a word.

It was pretty amazing, really, that no-one had noticed that something was 'on'. Over the preceding twelve months I had been gradually trimming the team size at Marauding Lodge, slowly chipping away. At nights, Maree and I had begun learning Swahili, through a former missionary who we had tracked down via contact with the Kenyan embassy. I kept thinking that someone would wake up to it soon. But no-one did, and when I gathered them all in the office one morning after the work was done and broke the news, it had something of a bombshell impact. From there I drove to the AJC and told them I would be handing in my licence in a month's time—because I was going to Africa.The news soon reached the media, as these things do, and with the speed of a spreading bushfire, the racing world was, at last, in on the 'secret'. In numerous interviews, I explained it as best I could to the media: 'Maree and I have developed a strong interest, indeed a passion, for wildlife in Africa. Basically it is our desire to become conservationists. We plan to use our skills and experience to help finance, care for and protect endangered species in Africa.' The reaction was extraordinary—and most of it immensely positive. Probably you could sum up the cards and letters and faxes this way: 'Wow! I wish I could do that!', although occasionally I was met by stunned silence as I talked it through with an owner.

I think in fact that a lot of people were rather inspired by what Maree and I had decided to do. That was pretty close to the greatest satisfaction that I got out of that whole turbulent time—that people were so positive in their reactions. I'd like to think that one or two of them were sparked enough by our decision to step closer to their own dreams. I'd imagined we'd have people telling us we were 'crazy' or 'bloody idiots', but we didn't, although one bloke did send us a letter and a map, outlining his opinion on why he thought we would 'fail' in Africa, based on theories about the climate, the deserts spreading further south and the effects on population. In a way he was right, but when you're fixed on an ideal, something you want to pursue, you certainly don't stop at the first hurdle.

For me, two of the great positives to emerge from this period were the gestures made by the major racing clubs. The AJC committee invited me as a special guest to their monthly luncheon—I was only the third person in twenty years to be afforded that honour. And the STC made a special presentation to Maree and me in the mounting enclosure on Golden Slipper day. I had expected nothing like that and was genuinely flattered.

It was surprising the number of prominent people who came to us and said things like, 'I admire you for what you're doing. I wish I could do it, or had the courage to do it.' The reality was that such a decision was easier for Maree and me than for most. We have no children. For people who have families, their first responsibility must be to that family. They don't have the luxury of being able to say to the kids, 'Look, we're nicking over to Africa now to save animals.'

Winding down in Sydney was a huge operation. In March–April 1995, I officially handed over my remaining Fox-owned horses, including the outstanding Big Dreams, to Ron Quinton, who had ridden Marauding for me when he won the Golden Slipper back in 1987. It was at Rosehill on our last day, George Ryder Stakes day, that Maree and I were feted as special guests of the Sydney Turf Club, and each of us given a memento of happy and successful years. 'I go with mixed feelings,' I told the people who had stayed in the grandstand for the official farewell, 'one of sorrow, one of excitement. I have in my mind a horse who, years ago, won a number of top races at this track—Time and Tide. It is now my time to leave, and the tide is high. Thank you very much . . . and goodbye.'

With associates, I shared more private thoughts: 'I've been a trainer for twenty-five years and I'm not going to be one in a few weeks' time,' I mused one day. 'This is what I'm used to doing. All of a sudden it's going to be gone. Like sitting on the edge of a plane waiting to jump—and the rope is cut. At first it's going to be like floating in space.'

Our plan was a broad one—to get over there, live a basic lifestyle, and investigate becoming involved in some useful project, whether on our own, or with others. In an interview with Channel 9's Johnny Tapp before we left, I said: 'The first time I went to Africa, it was for me. This time it's for the wildlife.' In another interview: 'The aim is to heighten our general knowledge and experience of the African continent . . . then we'd be looking to settle in Kenya or Tanzania to be involved in some small way with wildlife. We want to get to the broad spectrum of the people, the wildlife situation and the political scene.'

We were prepared to use our own money, or a fair bit of it anyway, to help save animals, or to at least make their situation better, and at the same time balance that by providing help to some of the people too. We knew it was going to be small, that what we were dreaming of was akin to the impact of a grain of sand on a big beach. And so we went . . .

***

Bumping up against enormous frustrations, gaining some enormous enjoyment, too, along the way, we gave it a go. Increasingly in Africa this time we ran into two hurdles which loomed impossibly high: firstly, to somehow find an avenue via which we could earn a living, and secondly, to be meaningfully involved in something that allowed us to feel like we were doing something worthwhile, getting somewhere.

In the travels of that year we found that the bureaucracy—just *the way* of things in Africa—made it terribly difficult for us to put down the positive footprint that we wanted to. There is an attitude over there that if you try to help someone, they tend to see you as a milking cow, to be ripped off. They home in on you like bees on the last spoonful of honey, and you end up helping no-one, and sort of weakening *yourself* in the process.

Excerpts from the diary of our trip, reproduced in the next chapter, illuminate pretty much how it was—the good and the not so good. We investigated a number of possibilities, including buying land in Zimbabwe attached to the Wangi National Park and setting up a tourist camp there. But when we got to Zimbabwe, friends there warned us of President Mugabe's early moves in the direction of taking the land back from white people and handing it over to his own people. Thankfully—in view of the increasingly grim developments along those exact lines in Zimbabwe in 1999–2000—we heeded the warnings and our own instincts.

As an individual, it's very hard to earn a living out of doing something positive with the wildlife in Africa. In our investigations we increasingly felt a bit like the little corner store competing against the big supermarket chain. All the established safari companies have the infrastructure and the client base that is beyond the reach of a couple of idealistic individuals starting out.

Yet there were many positive aspects of our trip that allowed us to bring back indelible memories of remarkable places, and remarkable animals. For all its difficulties, Africa is a place in which I generally feel comfortable, and I always find it fascinating. Somehow, the people are universally friendly, in spite of the poverty that exists. I feel a great sense of compassion for them. When you see the hopelessness and abject poverty of so many lives over there, you feel very deeply for the people.

Inevitably too, there is a desperate criminal element ever present on the fringe, adding an extra edge—but we have that here as well, of course. The difference is that we have nowhere near the numbers of people here, although I have a theory that the percentage of people who get into strife in a community is probably pretty much the same wherever you are in the world.

I subscribe to the idea that if your number is going to come up in life, well, it's going to come up. As long as you don't shorten the odds by doing outrageous things like jumping out of planes without a parachute in the hope of falling into a soft tree, then I reckon you've just got to live life normally, do unusual things, take the occasional reasonable chance. Just live. If it happens that your turn has come—there is nothing you can do about that. In the end your own personality guides you through life, so you might as well enjoy the ride and accept the fact that when you've had your crack at it, it's over—and you have to make room for someone else.

The Land Rover that carried us more than 42,000 kilometres along some of the worst roads in the world was a mixed blessing. In the main it did its job well, and travelling in our own vehicle gave us the freedom to wander off down back roads, and to places that would have been virtually impossible to reach any other way. But the difficulty was that our whole kit and caboodle—*our life*—was tied up in that car. Every single thing we had was in the Land Rover. As a result we were loath to stray too far from it because, Africa being the way it is, we realised that the chance of it being broken into, and everything being stolen, was very real. It was the only real drawback, that we couldn't park the wagon without worries for a day or two and go off wandering into the bush, looking for animals.

Subsequent events confirmed that what we had tried to do in Africa in 1995–96 probably wasn't for us—at that time, anyway. Soon after we made our decision and came back to Australia, Maree's mother became very ill. Suddenly there was a very genuine need for Maree to be back home, and eventually there was acceptance that for us to come back was the way it was meant to be at this time. But as far as I'm concerned—and I think Maree's the same—we're not finished with Africa yet. I certainly hope not—I don't want to just keep doing what I'm doing, then drop off the perch. My love for horses and Africa is such that both demand equal attention in my life.

We learned a lot, but probably came home with some regrets and a slightly 'empty' feeling. In so many ways it had been a voyage of discovery. We had roamed around in our Land Rover, mainly camping in the bush, with an occasional stay at a hotel. In the end it was not a particularly expensive exercise. Apart from the airfares, we lived pretty cheaply. The Land Rover was a US$45,000 investment when all kitted up, but when it was finally sold—after plenty of dramas over the fact that the papers were missing—we got US$39,000 for it. My quest to sell the Land Rover at times looked hopeless, but was finally guided through by a Nairobi solicitor, Anthony Gross, a very tenacious individual who shared our love of horses and was recommended to us by our good friend Pete Giraudo.

Dealing with the reality that we *hadn't* managed what we set out to do was not easy for me, and is not easy now. Since my boyhood days I have had the feeling that people don't think much of me, of my personality dragging me back. My inner view is that people see me as a distant, dour kind of person, short on 'personality'. Yeah, it's true that the press, and the public too, seem to have viewed me quite favourably, but I can say honestly that generally they have assessed me a fair bit more kindly than I have assessed myself.

Before the African trek, I had thought a great deal about what lay ahead, talked about it at length publicly. When we came home, I looked back on the experience and thought, well, what *have* I achieved? The real answer was: not much. That was tough to live with, very frustrating. I thought, jeeze, this is really bad for me. In the whole of my life to this point I have never really taken a backward step, and now I've had to retreat from something I really wanted to do. Excuses . . . justification . . . all that sort of stuff was easy to find. And at the end of the day, commonsense prevailed. But none of that took away from me the feeling that I had tackled something I passionately believed in only to be forced to step back from it. I had expounded all these ideals about helping wildlife, and yet I now had to come to terms with the fact that I hadn't really contributed anything of significance, except for throwing in some money here and there.

People say that I mark myself hard, that at least I 'gave it a go', which is more than most do. And I did—and we did. But it nags at me still. I find some consolation in the ongoing financial help we have been able to provide, and will continue to provide, such as to the black rhino program at Dubbo zoo, an initiative we support with great interest and enthusiasm.

Then I think to myself that it's really just small change thrown in a tray, like at church on a Sunday morning. And not enough to satisfy my 'God', I'm sorry to say.

CHAPTER EIGHTEEN

African Adventure

The trip of our lives took us 42,000 kilometres through the heartland of Africa, and lasted eleven months. We tangled with deserts, brutal roads, storms of unimaginable fury, and bureaucrats who drove us to distraction. Always, there were the animals to lift our spirits—magnificent, and vast in their diversity. Throughout it all, as an exercise in discipline and a record for 'posterity' of a special time in our lives, we kept a diary, faithfully recorded daily (well, almost!) whether our spirits were soaring or dipping low, as they did at times. This chapter and the next take you back with Maree and me to Africa, in fragments carefully selected from our joint writings, to give you a 'snapshot' of what it was like—of what we saw, and what we did.

Nairobi
24 April 1995
Maree: Seven forty-five a.m. Arrival in Nairobi. Forty-

seven years and forty-one years, respectively, of our previous lives have now effectively finished and a new life begins. Here's hoping the metamorphosis can be completed! What a start! It took six hours to get two suitcases of unaccompanied luggage through customs. Brian's patience in dealing with the eventual runaround was nothing short of a miracle. Finally, he came through with the cases and official paperwork, which had been stamped no less than sixteen times. Organised chaos would be a tame description.

26 April 1995
Maree: We have arrived in the lap of luxury, at the Windsor Golf and Country Club. Although it is only three years old it has been built in traditional old world English architecture. It is truly magnificent. The rooms have French doors opening out to a panoramic view of the golf course. Our friend, Marcus Russell, rang from Segera Ranch, which is 130 kilometres from Nanyuki, telling us they'd had an elephant in their front garden the previous evening.

Segera Ranch and Nanyuki

28 April 1995
Maree: Today we drove to Segera Ranch, where we were greeted by Marcus, Annabel, four dogs, two cats, a puppy, a baby vervet monkey, three genet kittens and an orphaned baby zebra.

29 April 1995
Maree: This morning we did a tour of the ranch, which for the most part looks like Africa untouched. We saw a lot of game: eland, zebra, impala, baboon, giraffe and eight elephants, which were probably the ones which

had invaded the garden on the previous evening while we were sleeping. Two of the elephants were large old bulls—the biggest we have seen for a long time.

Annabel is doing the rounds of her riding horses which are in yards behind a large hedge at the bottom of the garden. As I sit on the verandah writing, a troupe of baboon enter the garden, watching the horses through the hedge. One very large male becomes a bit too inquisitive and the dogs take exception and start to chase him. He takes a giant leap over the side hedge which would do justice to the horses in the Grand Annual Steeplechase at Warrnambool.

Evening: Annabel and I went for a walk this afternoon with the dogs, Mistari the zebra and Noogie the vervet, which clung to me all the way. We were soaked through in a torrential downpour. That is to say, all but Noogie, who was tucked up under my T-shirt.

Later: I just finished bottle-feeding the three genet kittens and they are now full of play. The kittens and Noogie put on quite an amusing show. Genets have the most beautiful coats, black spots and stripes over fawn and cream. Their eyes are the colour of topaz.

We first met Marcus in 1989. He was in the safari business at the time. We had our first private safari with him, travelling through Samburu, the Masai Mara and Tsavo National Parks. After giving up the safari work, he spent a few years running a wildlife sanctuary on his property at Malindi. The local politicians and squatters made it almost impossible for him, cutting down the fences and squatting on his land and threatening to shoot the two white rhino he had under his protection. One night armed bandits broke in and robbed and terrorised him and Annabel. All these events appeared to have been set up by a local politician who had more than a passing interest in the property. After getting no assistance from the local authorities, Marcus decided to move the animals off to safer areas and sell the land.

1 May 1995
Maree: While the sun was out this morning, we went for a two-hour walk, along the river and back up the ridge to the house. There was not much game about but we saw zebra, eland, Thompson's gazelle, Grant's gazelle and a lone bull elephant. Later in the afternoon, Brian and Marcus headed out and came across a lioness on a kill (zebra), only two kilometres from the house.

3 May 1995
Brian: It was a beautiful morning, sunny, the grass a lush green after the recent rains. We were looking at a group of over twenty-three giraffe and a herd of elephants, moving out of the trees, about a mile to our right-hand side, with the snow-capped Mt Kenya looking fantastic as a backdrop to this beautiful scene, and then amazingly a telephone call came through on the radio in our 4 x 4 from *A Current Affair* TV program in Australia.

4 May 1995
Brian: We left the house early this morning to go to the north of the ranch, where a number of elephants were harassing a cattle herder, and found a big bull there when we arrived. Marcus frightened him away with a number of live shotgun charges. He took off very quickly, running in a straight line, away from us, and then disappeared into the bush three-quarters of a mile from us—without once looking back. We got bogged on the way back (a regular event for us since we've been here!).

8 May 1995

Maree: Marcus, Brian and I had a great drive this afternoon, down around the southern end of the ranch. We went to look at a leopard bait which Marcus had put high in a tree beside a waterfall. When we arrived, we found the bait had been taken, but by a lion as well as a leopard. It's hard to say which had gotten there first, but there was a lot of spoor [tracks] around the ground at the base of the tree, and the tree itself was clawed to pieces. It's a pity we missed the action.

We drove over to a rocky outcrop on the side of a ridge which afforded magnificent views of the Segera River and valley beyond. Behind us was a large plain with good-sized herds of impala, oryx, zebra (including Grevey's) and a lone female ostrich. We could see large herds of zebra and elephants in the distance. We drove amongst a herd of elephants and spent half an hour in their company. The mothers and babies were to our left and herd bulls to our right. It is so very easy to become mesmerised by them. Just on dusk we encountered a herd of buffalo.

9 May 1995

Maree: The elephant was in the garden again last night, around 3.45 a.m. The old bugger seems determined to get at the pepper trees, considered to be a delicacy.

12 May 1995

Maree: This afternoon we did a drive around the northern end of the property, and saw the biggest herd of eland we have ever seen—well over 100, including lots of babies and one massive bull. He was huge and 'blue' with age. When we came up to them, they were walking almost single file along a ridge, forming a silhouette against the skyline. An unforgettable sight. We saw lots of elephants as well and had a confrontation with a cranky old female, who charged us a couple of times, coming within 4.5 metres of the vehicle.

A short while afterwards, we were racing across an open plain, chasing a herd of eland. I was standing up at the back of the pick-up filming the chase when we hit a hole, probably a warthog den, coming to an abrupt halt. I was slammed against the roll-bar and gave my ribs a very hard whack. I got such a shock, I was incapable of uttering a word, even to swear!

13 May 1995

Maree: It was a very long day today and a very full one. Annabel came home from her morning ride with a two-week-old baby zebra draped across the pommel of her saddle. I had been unable to go as my ribs were extremely sore from the incident the previous day. She had found the foal alone and seriously injured. Its top jaw had been broken, probably from a kick, it had deep puncture wounds to the neck and hindquarters, and was in deep shock. After Brian had given it a couple of injections to ease the pain so we could examine it more closely, we came to the inevitable conclusion that it could not be saved.

We spent the rest of the day on the neighbouring property—20,000 acres of wild country owned by Ivan Tomlinson. We stopped at an incredible oasis surrounded by amazing rock formations. One huge stone pillar balanced above the waterfall surrounded by huge smooth boulders, coloured copper, silver and gold in the subdued afternoon light. The continual flow of the river had smoothed and burnished these large rocks, exposing the minerals, which gave off such glorious colours. From here the river spilt over the fall into a large pool surrounded by palm trees and grassed areas and inhabited by hippos.

15–17 May 1995

Brian: Today [15 May] we set out for Nairobi to buy a vehicle, a Land Rover Discovery. Eleven kilometres outside of Nanyuki, we had a flat tyre, and on changing it, found the spare one deflating as well. We drove back on the slowly deflating one. All the shops in Nanyuki were closed. The President of Kenya, Daniel Arap Moi, was in town.

We arrived in Nairobi at 6.00 p.m. What a 'hellhole' it is to drive in! It was getting dark, lightly raining—crawling congested traffic with basically 'Rafferty's Rules' and copious clouds of diesel smoke. I shudder to think how much worse it will get in the next ten years.

The next two days in Nairobi were a complete waste of time because of the non-availability of documents of ownership for the vehicle—yet they wanted us to pay over our money saying that things take time in Kenya and to 'trust' them to get it done! It was explained to them that when it comes to our money (US$40,000)—even if it is in Kenya—we do it 'our' way!

23 May 1995

Brian: Today we went out to hunt a male buffalo [females are not hunted] as part of the quota system to sell for game meat. [The hunting and killing of animals is anathema to us; we were observers, not participants, in the hunt. However, I believe that to understand something fully, you have to experience it. All farmers in this area have a hunting quota system, strictly controlled by Kenyan Wildlife Service, on game moving through their farms. The purpose is twofold: to control numbers and to provide meat for local people.] Buffalo sells for about ninety shillings a kilo, and this ranch is allowed to hunt ten in a year, its quota determined by Kenya Wildlife Service. It has been well documented that these animals are among the most dangerous in Africa. Bearing that in mind, and this being my first hunt, it was with a degree of trepidation that I went along. These animals' habitat is very thick bush, with visibility varying from three to eighteen metres. It usually takes at least two or three shots of heavy calibre (.458) to kill them; they are very tough animals, aggressive and dangerous when wounded in this terrain.

We found a herd, got out on foot and with the breeze blowing away from the herd, toward us, we started to stalk, to try and select an older bull. This proved very difficult to do, as they kept moving. Whenever we got close enough, the cows got in the way. The morning continued; a lot of walking, getting close, the buffalo moving away, and us tracking them again. Zebra proved a nuisance, as they kept running and alerting the buffalo whenever they saw us. At midday—after more than four hours of walking, crouching, hiding, waiting—we found a group of five bulls, among a herd of elephants, about a mile and a half away, on a ridge in scrub. We crept up on them, so close to the elephants that we could hear their stomachs rumbling. We were downwind of them, but unfortunately for us, fortunately for the buffalo, they somehow detected our presence and took off.

We followed a small winding *donga* [creek] bed covered, in a lot of places, by bushes. We were following some fresh tracks when suddenly a bull which had been hiding burst with an explosive crash from the undergrowth, no more than three metres from us, and he took off up a ridge into scrub. It was our good fortune that he decided not to come our way; he would have flattened us before we knew what hit us. All morning, as well as walking, I had been carrying a 7mm Magnum rifle (to be used as protection in an emergency) which was getting fairly heavy. Marcus and the four Africans ran after the buffalo. Unfit and feeling all of my forty-eight years, I could hardly pick my feet up. If a buffalo had charged me, I would have had to cop it sweet. I struggled after them . . .

Into the thick scrub, everyone was ahead of me when I heard water splashing—by a large animal—in scrub to my left. I eventually got Marcus's attention and alerted him to it, and he came back quickly. It was a bull buffalo, rolling in a small, muddy waterhole. Marcus got off one shot from his .458 which hit the animal behind the shoulder. Before he could fire again, the buffalo wheeled and crashed off through the scrub. We followed his tracks and blood trail for the next hour and the animal circled—right back to where we had left the vehicle parked in the bush. We had a rest and a drink of water at last, and by this time I didn't mind admitting that physically, I'd 'had it'.

Marcus and the others continued to track the animal and I drove the vehicle to a prearranged place to meet up with them a couple of hours later. Unfortunately they didn't find the buffalo, and in spite of constant searching over the next couple of days, it was never found. I felt uneasy with the situation, having caused his pain by spotting him earlier. I realise that the reality of life is that animals will be killed. But I don't like it, and if it must be done, then it must be done quickly.

24 May 1995
Brian: Today is my forty-eighth birthday and I am going out with Marcus, game cropping under the Kenya Wildlife Service quota system allocated to the ranch. The animals required are zebra and a bull eland. We started out on zebra first, mainly males from bachelor groups, although on this day, one female was cropped and found not to be in foal. Marcus is a very good shot and all the animals were dead within seconds of being shot, except for one male. Although he'd been shot in the correct position (just behind the shoulder), he didn't die quickly and needed four shots.

In the afternoon we went looking for a bull eland. They are very big and magnificent animals, especially the older bulls. We came onto a large herd of about sixty that afternoon; they were very alert and ran away very smartly, so it was not easy to select a good bull and get a good shot at it. After tracking them through low thorn bushes for one and a half hours, Marcus decided to circle around to the north. This proved a good move as we eventually came upon a group of males. An animal about fourteen to fifteen years old was selected by Marcus.

It was sundown after a long afternoon, and interesting to note the behaviour change in the six Africans on the hunt. Their spirits were greatly elevated by the success and they became quite cheerful—after having been very subdued until then. The eland was felled with one shot from a .458 calibre to the shoulder and finished with a pistol shot to the head. Mercifully things were over very quickly for him.

25 May 1995
Brian: Maree has started painting animals on ostrich

eggs, also on flat stones. They look very good, even though it's the first time she has done them.

28 May 1995
Brian: We visited a couple, the Kenyons (strange name coincidence), old white farmers who have farmed cattle and sheep here for over forty years. The wife is on the Land Council and we made enquiries about leasing land here, which she said would be very difficult, us being non-residents of Kenya. She confirmed our instincts, since we've been here, that the government and a lot of the people are not happy with white people (*wazungu*), owning land of 'theirs' and would prefer to see the existing ones off it. It's apparent this will make it very difficult for us to do what we came here to do—occupy some scenic land, build a residence, do a bit of tourism, maybe with a few cattle to keep things ticking over, be involved in some worthwhile animal conservation, and help some young people with their education. We both want to be in the bush amongst African animals. Hopefully when we get to know the country better than we do now, things will look more positive.

29 May 1995
Brian: We went to the north end of the property today at Mutare to hunt six male zebra for game meat—to fill an order from Delamere Estates. We were very fortunate while there to encounter a big herd of over 200 elephants on the Mutare creek. Nearby we had a very interesting experience with elephant behaviour: we were upwind of the leading groups of the herd when, from about 400 metres away, two females charged when we got out of the vehicle—obviously on scent alone as they couldn't have seen us very well from that

distance, being partly disguised by bush as well. They came on very quickly, ears back, trunks curled under. This had a feeling of deadly intent rather than the more normal 'mock' charge, which usually stops short, with a lot of noise. We got back in the vehicle very quickly. Marcus was intrigued by it, declaring they would have killed anyone on foot, with that intent.

30 May 1995
Brian: On Tuesday night we went out to hunt some of Thompson's gazelle for game meat—as usual selecting males from bachelor groups. We used a spotlight and a .22 calibre rifle. None of these hunts was able to commence without there being a Muslim among the African workers, to cut the animal's throat after it went down.

31 May 1995
Maree: This evening we went for a night drive, a totally different experience to day driving as the animals react so differently. Buffalo, which normally bolt when you get to within 45–90 metres, are so dazzled by the lights of the vehicle and the spotlight that you can get right up to them. We drove in among a herd of about thirteen and seventeen and they milled around in a confused manner, colliding with one another as well as the vehicle. The smell was incredibly strong.

Later, we sighted our first aardvark, which shot into its burrow as we approached. Nearing the hole we could see him peering up at us. We bent over to get a better look just as he kicked up a huge cloud of dirt, in which he made good his escape. We saw another, which we followed for a while and its waddling action reminded us of a bald wombat. We also saw two aardwolves.

12 June 1995
Brian: Marcus came back with a report that an elephant, a female, had been found standing in the Ewaso Ngiro River on Ivan Tomlinson's ranch, and appeared to be injured as it had been there for a number of days. We went over with him to have a look at the situation. We could get within four metres of her and she wouldn't charge—the reason being apparent later. We threw grass into the water near her but she wasn't interested.

Eventually Ivan made the decision to shoot her, and although we knew it was going to be done, the swiftness of his action caught us by surprise. I would say that she was dead in two seconds, from a shot straight into the brain. Although it was a sad experience to see one's first elephant kill, it was mercifully swift. She didn't know what hit her. The next thing to do was to get her out of the water and see what the problem was [her back leg was infected], and also to remove her ivory, which had to be handed into the Kenya Wildlife Service. The lions and hyenas will be here tonight, and will eat well. For a while something else will live a bit longer.

19 June 1995
Brian: Success at last! We flew from Nanyuki to Nairobi today to buy a new four-wheel drive vehicle, after two months of being dependent on other people to move around and the feeling of 'getting nowhere'. We took delivery of a brand new Land Rover Defender County TDI 300 station wagon from an independent dealer who imported vehicles into Kenya. It exceeded our expectations, with air conditioning, power steering, radio, cassette deck, etc. The price was also good for Kenya, KSH 2.2 million (US$42,300). The same vehicle at the

official Land Rover dealer in Nairobi, Coopers Motors Corporation, was listed at KSH 3.2 million.

Samburu National Park

2 July 1995

Maree: It is always a wonderful sight to watch families of elephants playing and meeting in the wide shallow waters of the Ewaso Ngiro River. The tiny babies have such 'joi de vivre', as they roll and frolic along the bank.

Meru National Park

3 July 1995

Maree: Meru is well worth it, a truly beautiful park. There are many fast-flowing rivers and streams winding through forested areas and across the open, grassy plains. The roads and river crossings throughout the park are well maintained by the KWS. It was in this park that George and Joy Adamson did most of their work with lions—Elsa, star in *Born Free*, being the most famous. George was murdered by poachers just outside the northern perimeter a few years ago and the park has been considered unsafe for tourists since, hence the strong presence of the KWS within.

4 July 1995

Maree: We saw a herd of around 150 elephants making their way down towards the swamp. We sat on the airstrip and watched the passing parade. They almost danced past us, with thoughts of glorious mudbaths uppermost on their minds, as they spilled out into the swamp.

We decided the best 'safari' we could undertake that afternoon would be to sit on the patio in front of the bar, with a cold 'Tusker' (beer) in hand—and be thoroughly entertained by these magnificent creatures playing and cavorting right in front of us. They were still there well after dark, evidenced by the trumpeting and squealing that continued on until late in the night.

A sight like this is by pure chance only. A group of French tourists who had arrived that morning and gone out on a game drive had missed the whole magnificent show.

Solio Ranch

8 July 1995

Brian: We met the manager, a Mr Bristow. No first name was forthcoming. He at first seemed a bit distant in his attitude but nonetheless invited us into his office. We showed him our letter of recommendation from Ian Denny, director of Western Plains Zoo in Dubbo, and some photos of the black rhino there. He then spoke quite expansively on the black rhino situation in Kenya, naming Solio and Nairobi National Park as the places where the animals have done the best. Sixty-six rhino have been relocated from Solio in Kenya since the program's inception in 1967. Black rhino always remain the property of Kenya and are not owned by individuals. White rhino can be owned by individuals. The numbers of rhino today in Solio are: black rhino forty-six, white rhino fifty-seven.

Nanyuki

11 July 1995

Maree: We received the most pleasant surprise when we went to Nyayo House to get our visas extended. We expected a long wait, loads of paperwork and, of course, the usual fee. But, lo and behold, all it took was one form filled in, a stamp in the passport—and we are now at liberty to roam around Kenya for a further three months. All of it done in twenty minutes. We returned to Nanyuki the following day.

28 July 1995
Maree: We left for Nairobi today to buy our camping kit. Gary McIntyre, who owns 'Beach and Bush', had a special bedroll made up for us which fits neatly into the back of the Land Rover. We also bought a shower bag, two directors chairs, a table and mosquito net. From there we went to Nakumart where we bought a gas lamp, cooker, sheets, blankets, pots, etc. The night of the 28th we camped in the garden at Pete Girado's house, giving ourselves a practice run.

5–29 July (recalled)
Brian: During this period we stayed outside Nanyuki, at Jamie Roberts' house. Jamie kindly allowed us to stay while we awaited a bank guarantee to enable us to get a 'Carnet de Passage' from the Automobile Association for our long safari. We had a very interesting experience with wildlife behaviour while there. Every night, about two hours after sundown, an eerie, piercing, screeching noise would start in the trees around the house. It sounded like it belonged to one of those giant birds of the dinosaur age. Jamie was away at the time, and it took us a few days to establish that the noise was coming from a tree hyrax, which are nocturnal and live in the forest among high trees. We had seen plenty of rock hyrax and thought that they were the only species. After a couple of weeks you start to get used to the noise.

Masai Mara
29 July 1995
Maree: We drove to the Masai Mara game reserve today,

hoping to camp there for three days. After a lot of 'kerfuffling' around we finally bedded down for the night, convinced that our camping technique could only improve!

31 July 1995
Maree: This morning we spent three hours driving around the Mara in search of rhino. There are supposed to be about thirty inside the park. Later, we headed for Willie Roberts' camp, about forty kilometres from where we are staying.

Willie Roberts' camp: The guy who looks after the rhino took us out to see them. They have nine rhino—five male, three female, one with a tiny two-month-old calf. They were flown up from South Africa last September, then trucked from Nairobi to the park. They are free to roam around the reserve during the day, then herded into *bomas* for the night. They are all very quiet except for one male who had apparently chased a guard up a tree the previous day. It was wonderful to be able to walk amongst them in the open reserve. We got to within three metres. While we were filming, the mother lay down in front of us and fed the baby. It was incredible.

Ten minutes after we left there, we saw five cheetah together in one group, hunting Thompson's gazelles. I was so happy to see them, as cheetah have always been very special animals to me.

2 August 1995
Maree: The shower: I couldn't complete this little excursion without a description of the shower. The shower bag itself was over half a metre long with a further half a metre of chain above it, which meant it

needed to be hung over a branch at least three metres high to enable someone to stand underneath. The young guy, however, failed to calculate this and set it up over a rather low branch so that the nozzle was about half a metre above the ground—just great if you happened to be a midget!

I overcame this minor setback by sitting in my plastic washtub under the shower, which had only one covered-in side—so I had the most wonderful 270 degree panoramic view of the open savanna whilst relaxing in the 'tub'! I amaze even myself at my adaptability and my rapidly declining sense of dignity!!!

Nairobi

2 August 1995

Brian: Humour, like tragedy, is never far away in Africa. While seated at the Fair View Hotel in Nairobi for dinner one night, we couldn't help but hear the conversation at a nearby table. Fortyish American (fading soapie star type) to young African waiter after studying the menu: 'What is the catch of the day?'

The confident reply from the young waiter, 'It is fish, sir!'

The news that comes about Sydney racing since we have been here is, it seems, of one sensation after another. I know that I wouldn't be happy there and feel that my departure was well timed. I don't miss it.

El Karama Ranch

7 August 1995

Maree: Once again, we have a campsite all to ourselves, and as we write, we can hear lions calling. My camp cooking has taken a turn for the better as I managed to provide curried sausages and rice—a vast improvement on canned soup. We set up our bedroll and mosquito net in the *banda* (African hut) and had a very comfortable night's sleep. I'm not too keen on the bats in the 'loo' though!

An Indian shop owner in Nanyuki has lined up a job for Brian: training local polo horses. What an opportunity!!!

10 August 1995
Maree: I had my first encounter with a snake. I was on my way to the loo (ninety metres behind the banda) when a green mamba shot past my foot, less than one-third of a metre away. I was so glad that it was in just as much of a hurry to get away from me as I was from it! All desire to go to the loo was very quickly forgotten as I backpedalled to the hut.

11 August 1995
Brian: Last night the hyenas called constantly—until 5.00 a.m. this morning. There was a big yellow moon and a clear sky last night. Maybe that's what got them going—the moon.

15–17 August 1995
Brian: Dealing with Mr Mwange, bank manager for Barclays Bank, Hurlingham, is about as easy as winning the Melbourne Cup with a three-legged, blind horse. Although very pleasant in manner, he and his staff are totally incompetent, driving us and our bank manager from Sydney, Joe Letto, nearly around the bend.

Amboseli

18 August 1995
Brian: We set off on another mini-safari, this time to

Amboseli—and if we thought the road to the Mara had problems, this was worse. The road to Namanga had craters in the bitumen and corrugation in the dirt. We arrived at the campsite about 3.30 p.m. and wrangled with the Masai for a while over the cost of the campsite and firewood before settling in. The campsite looked like an old cattle *boma*, rather rough by daylight, but in the softer light of the evening, it proved to be more pleasant. Private, at least.

19 August 1995
Brian: This afternoon, the sunset was a spectacular sight. As we drove through the park we had a wonderful view of Kilimanjaro to our left, her snow cap taking on the colour of soft pink icing reflected by the brilliant sunset on our right. I have always wanted to see this and it was not disappointing. The sight of a family of elephants on a hill, silhouetted against a fireball sunset, was breathtaking.

Tsavo West

20 August 1995
Maree: On the move again—this time to Tsavo West. A hitch occurred when we did not realise that we needed a police escort along the road between Amboseli and the Chulyu gate at Tsavo West. We arrived at the police post, which was a barricade across the road attended by armed, out-of-uniform policemen. They told us we had to take an armed escort with us—but the problem was, the car was packed to the rafters and there was no room for a third person. I wasn't keen to have a guy with an AK47 in the vehicle with us anyway. You couldn't be sure that these were legitimate police—with no uniforms or badges. Luckily for us, another vehicle pulled up and it was decided that the

guard could go in that vehicle, and we would follow in convoy. Shortly after setting off, the escort vehicle shot ahead of us—and that was the last we saw of our escort!

Mzima Springs is an incredible oasis in the middle of this vast area. The pure spring water, filtered by vast areas of volcanic rock, flows into large pools, crystal clear, surrounded by trees and dense vegetation. There is an underground observation tank in one of the hippo pools where we watched the hippos swim underwater as we sat eating our lunch.

On a drive to a tented camp to the south of Mzima Springs (Finch Hatton Camp) we were fortunate to see a huge male leopard. We disturbed him as he was stalking three young waterbuck. On our approach, the leopard turned back across the road in front of us, making its way into the cover of the acacia trees. The three waterbuck followed at a safe distance, intent on seeing just where the predator had gone.

24 August 1995
Brian: At night as we sit by the fire, the elephants at the waterhole nearby growl and call out to each other as they come in for water, and sound extremely close. The 'elephant talk' goes on as we go to sleep in the back of the Land Rover.

25 August 1995
Brian: Since the bad poaching days of the late eighties, the elephant numbers are increasing and there are a lot of young ones here, although interestingly, some of the older ones are still a bit edgy when vehicles come near them. Obviously they haven't forgotten their terrible experiences.

26 August 1995

Brian: Today is the first time since we've been in Africa that I have had an uneasy feeling about giving everything up in Australia to come here—as we learn more of how people in a country like this think and about our own limitations in wildlife. There is a great need by most of the people—but a great greed by people in positions of power (at the expense of their own people). So, any project that may be successfully implemented by people with good intentions is eventually sucked financially dry by this greed. If we can't implement something that is self-funding, and if we put in too much of our own finances, we will eventually go broke—and need help ourselves! At this stage I can't see how we can make a career out of wildlife. Tourism is one obvious way of funding a worthwhile animal project, but there seems now to be more supply than demand in that area. Maybe what I am writing is a natural touch of homesickness. However . . . we have at this point decided to travel on and keep an open mind until April of next year—at which time we will either decide to go home to Australia or feel that we are qualified to stay here and carry on with our original wildlife conservation ambitions.

Nanyuki

28 August 1995

Brian: 'Breakthrough Day!' We have our guarantee to get the 'carnet de passage' to travel through Africa. It has been two months of waiting; under the circumstances it feels like a great achievement. Tomorrow we go to the Automobile Association to hopefully conclude the exercise and be given the carnet.

29 August 1995
Brian: While I was waiting in the bank, Richard Leakey, a world famous conservationist (his parents found the earliest evidence of humans in Africa) and founder of Kenya Wildlife Service, sat down beside me. I decided to ask his advice on the likely direction of Kenya for the next two years, and our best way of becoming involved in wildlife. He generally confirmed the fears and doubts of which I wrote on 26 August, which is interesting. He said that tourism had a good future in the long term but in the short term, it would suffer because of the political situation and the negative publicity it would attract. People are turning to crime more and more, because they cannot find jobs in the failing system. Corruption by local authorities plunders any worthwhile project which is financially successful; giving people charity is eventually taken for granted by them. It seems, therefore, that investment and total commitment in this country would not be wise. That leaves us 'out on a limb' at this stage.

30 August 1995
Brian: Today I have taken the Land Rover to CMC, the Nairobi dealership, for the 10,000 kilometres service. I have to sit there and amuse myself from 7.45 a.m. until 5.00 p.m. as it is too far to go back to Pete Giraudo's place in Langata and to then return in the afternoon. Still, I get through the day okay and it doesn't seem to be so bad. Africa has taught me to be patient already!

31 August 1995
Brian: It's 'Departure Day' from Kenya, two months later than we originally planned, and we are very happy to be on our way.

Tanzania

1 September 1995

Brian: As we approach Moshi, Kilimanjaro looms out of the clouds, very close—with much more snow around the top than on the Kenyan side, as we had viewed it from Amboseli a couple of weeks ago. The mountain looks simply spectacular. It's not hard to understand how an uneducated and unsophisticated people of many years ago thought God lived there. I would have felt the same way myself . . . it just gives you that kind of feeling.

2 September 1995

Lake Malawi: As night falls there is the sound nearby of native singing and drums with dancing—and a few hours later, they dance down to the water's edge on the beach and along it and away into the distance.

3 September 1995

Brian: Today, Sunday, is an idyllic day for us—starting with the most beautiful sunrise over the smooth waters of the lake which we can see from our bed in the back of the Land Rover. We see fishermen going out early in their canoes with a small net, two in each canoe—and diving over the side periodically with the net to catch the fish.

5 September 1995

Brian: I got 'done' by an armed soldier for speeding at the South Lawanga River, which has a massive new bridge over it, with only a single one-way lane, with a speed limit of ten kilometres per hour. As we reach the other side an armed soldier with an automatic weapon asks me to get out of the car, points to the sign, and says

I am charged with speeding and will have to report to a police station at a small town 100 kilometres back in the direction from which we have just come—to pay the fine. I ask him if I can pay the fine here, and he says no as we might lay a complaint because he can't give us a receipt. So I say that we don't need a receipt, and he says the fine is 20,000 Zam. Kwacha. (The exchange rate the day before in Chipata was US$1 to 928 Zam.KW.) We say that we haven't got that much money in Kwacha, and ask if the equivalent in US dollars will do. He says, 'Okay, forty dollars US.' We explain to him that that's double the fine in Kwacha. He thinks for a moment and then says, 'Okay, twenty dollars is fine', and we are on our way. I have no problems with the deal; I had broken the speed limit and what followed was simply the way business is usually done in Africa.

Harare

7 September 1995

Brian: In Harare, while stopped at a set of traffic lights, we had to wait while what appeared to be a President Mugabe motorcade went past. It looked a bit like an invasion, motorcycle cops stretched ahead of the string of limousines, support trucks carrying eight soldiers, each with automatic weapons, and wearing frosted silver helmets (like something out of 'Dr Who'), plus an assortment of other vehicles, all moving very fast. Someone is obviously very nervous!

South Africa—Touchstone Game Park

25 September 1995

Brian: We saw a male nyala for the first time. They are an attractive antelope, a bit like a bongo but much darker, with quite a thick coat. Apart from that we saw steenbok, impala, wildebeest, kudu, etc. The next day we were much more fortunate and saw seven white rhino, one fleeing with her calf running in front of her, as is their way. The black rhino are the opposite, with the baby running behind the mother when fleeing.

Berg En Dal Camp, Kruger National Park

27 September 1995

Brian: The manager of the camp, John M. Carter, and his wife Marion are friends of ours, and while having dinner with them the previous evening, they sprung a great surprise on us. John said, 'How would you guys like to go out on a rhino relocation capture with the National Parks staff in the morning?' So this morning we picked up the vet Kobus Roth and staff and moved out into the bush looking for rhino.

Five hundred metres down the road from where we were standing a black rhino cow and calf burst out of the bush and crossed the road in a rush—the helicopter following at a height of about 100 metres. A few minutes later a call came through on the radio, and we all took off in a rush, through the bush, to one that had been brought down by a tranquilliser dart. It was a two-year-old female calf, quite big nonetheless. The mother had been hit by a dart also, but it had failed to work. She ran on and wisely was left for another day. They didn't want to stress her too much. The handlers and the vets went to work on the downed rhino—the handlers applying buckets of water and wet bags, also head and leg ropes and a blindfold as the vets administered a recovery antidote. For a few seconds there was great concern as the animal had a muscle seizure from the effects of the drug. One of the park staff jumped on her with both feet heavily—to get her heart going again. She recovered quickly and was soon back on her feet with what seemed to be 100 people hanging onto the head and leg ropes. Eventually they managed to manoeuvre the rhino into the loading crate, and the capture was complete.

The purpose of the exercise was to relocate rhino to a new reserve, up near the Botswana border—and away from this boundary of the park where there is danger from poachers.

Skukuza

28 September 1995

Maree: It was an amazing feeling as we walked across planks over the top of the *bomas*—and looked down on white rhino to our left and black rhino to our right. White rhino require larger *bomas* than the black in the initial settling-down period, but they can be moved into smaller spaces after a couple of weeks. It can take this long to bring them onto their feed; they are more difficult than the black. If they are not eating after two to three weeks they are released.

We also visited the elephant *boma* where six four- to five-year-old elephants were housed. These had been orphaned during culling operations in the park and were apparently 'spared' to be sold privately. As much as I try to understand this, I just can't agree. In fact, I find it difficult to agree with or understand culling in the first place. In Kruger, I had the impression the elephants were culled far more than necessary, primarily to keep the park looking 'pretty'. Even though elephants can do enormous damage, it has been proved that without man's interference, Mother Nature has a way of sorting it out in the long run. This is done either by drought or the elephants themselves curtailing their breeding—much the same as the kangaroo does in Australia.

Secondly, I believe that if culling is absolutely necessary, it would be kinder to wipe out an entire family group than have the three to five year olds left, to be sold as 'pets' later on. They have little chance of growing up normal after witnessing the slaughter of their families. Anybody who questions the kinship among elephants need only stop and watch a family group for a couple of hours to become totally convinced that the family structure is as strong, and in some cases stronger, than in human families. As with humans, a group of young can grow up delinquent without the matriarchal influence, teachings and guidance.

Thirdly, what is the purpose (long-term) of buying a baby elephant? What happens when one of these 'pets' is a five-ton full-grown? Do you send it on to a zoo, or release it back to the wild—unable to care for itself, having missed out on the early education on such things as where to find water, how to vary feeding in order to maintain variety and constant supply, etc?

Chapter Nineteen

Into the Wet

We battled on, good days following not so good, with breathtaking moments in enough abundance to keep our spirits and faith high, even if we sensed that the chances of achieving what we had set out to do on a permanent basis in Africa seemed to be slipping away. As the year advanced (late December 1995 and to early January 1996) we headed into the 'wet'—to the period when Africa's great storms rolled in daily with clockwork precision, adding drama to the experience, and a new challenge for the traveller. The 'gap' that exists in our diary days here (in January 1996) is covered in Chapter One—the story of our troubled return to Nanyuki, and the flight over the Aberdares and the Masai Mara which sent our spirits soaring . . .

Hoedsprit

29 September 1995

Maree: At the cheetah sanctuary, it was a rude shock to

be treated as a 'tourist', i.e., to experience a minibus tour of the enclosures complete with a tour guide uttering nonsense and childish jokes. One 'fellow tourist' observing a serval cat remarked, 'Look, it sits just like a cat.' What did she expect?

30 September 1995
Maree: What a shit of a day! We effectively drove 860 kilometres for nothing, heading for Sun City, hoping to stay in the nearby National Park. I was livid with myself for missing a turn-off which added about 100 kilometres to the trip. As it turned out, this was only a *minor* 'bitch' in the entire day. We came within a fraction of running out of fuel, driving for many, many kilometres on 'empty', and feeling very uneasy by the time we finally reached a small town and got directions to the nearest petrol station from the local cop. We then headed for the National Park—but, of course, it was absolutely full up.

Hluluwe Park

6 October 1995
Brian: Today we went into Hluluwe Park, and on entry were immediately into a white rhino 'sightathon', seeing three grazing along the base of a hill 400 metres to our right—and for the day a grand total of twenty-five. The most interesting thing of all, though, happened late in the day. We observed up close (thirty metres) a female calf, less than two years old, grazing with a mature bull rhino, with no sign of the mother anywhere. It was interesting to see that when he grazed away from her, she would hastily get back close to him, probably for security.

Durban

7 October 1995

Maree: The plan was to tour the battlefields around Rorke's Drift, but it was not without hiccups. We got ourselves lost and finished up in the black homelands, and I started to worry when I saw six freshly dug graves in the front of one house, followed by some very odd looks from the locals. We turned around and got out of there quick smart. This 'Mother of all Picnics' (our trek) can be a pain in the arse at times. We seem to have a natural talent for taking the longest way possible to travel the shortest distance.

8 October 1995

Brian: We camped last night in a town called Ladysmith and today went to visit Rorke's Drift battle site where 450 British soldiers fought 4000 Zulu warriors at this small outpost. The museum at the site was very good and showed graphically how the battle was fought on 22 January 1879.

18 October 1995

Brian: Onwards we travel, through the Karoo, heading for Mountain Zebra National Park. We do a game drive as soon as we arrive there. Although there is not a lot of game, we see the mountain zebra, which seems to be a cross between a Burchell's and a Grevey's zebra and outstandingly marked in rich colours. We also see our first springbok, which looks very similar to a Thompson's gazelle, although the horns are different and they run with their heads lowered, and they also 'pronk' [springing into the air with a stiff-legged action] about two metres high.

En route to Port Elizabeth

19 October 1995

Brian: By sheer chance the BBC World Service came on the radio, with the announcement that Red Rum, the champion English steeplechaser, had died aged thirty years. A phenomenal horse. News, too, that the Australian Jockey Club had been taken over by the New South Wales Government. It was quite a shock for us, the idea that the oldest governing body in Australian racing was no more.

Addo Elephant Park

20 October 1995

Brian: Two big bulls were walking towards the road, angling to our position on it. We drove to a bend where we estimated that they would cross. A few minutes later they came out of the bush towards us and passed by only a few feet away, not deviating from their original line. It was exciting to be so close to such a large wild animal without being threatened.

Tsitsikama National Park

24 October 1995

Maree: We have become quite diurnal, waking at daylight (5.00 a.m.) and going to bed between 7.30 and 8.30 p.m.—reminiscent of our previous life in the horse industry! It was a lovely morning, a bit cool, but clear and fresh so we decided to enjoy one of the many walks within the park. The wooden pathway wound around the foreshore before ascending into thick bushland, or rather, rainforest. We explored some deep and interesting caves along the way. The pathway concluded at the mouth of the Stormsriver where a suspension bridge crossed over the wide, pristine expanse of water.

At Keuboomsrivier we sat down to enjoy a beer when we spotted a large pod of dolphins, playing and feeding in the surfline (our camp was only thirty metres from the beach). We watched fascinated as the fifty to sixty dolphins fed on the large schools of fish and body-surfed the waves. The water here is so clear it is almost transparent, and we could actually watch the dolphins under the waves.

Wilderness National Park

26 October 1995

Brian: The sun feels good as we have a couple of beers by the river and not long after we settle down, along comes a steam train, crossing the bridge 200 metres away. It looks really good with its brass shining, chugging slowly over the bridge with about half a dozen passenger carriages in tow. I love steam trains as they seem to be alive. They are a very rare sight these days and just for a moment it makes one feel like a kid again.

Simonstown

2 November 1995

Maree: We walk into town and investigate some of the small shops, and spend a few hours in the Duke of Norfolk pub. We find the people very friendly. As soon as they hear our Australian accent they start up a conversation. They tell us they have been starved of overseas 'guests' during the apartheid era.

3 November 1995

Maree: This morning we made our way down towards the Cape of Good Hope. We climbed up to the lighthouse, a burst of exercise which really got the pulse racing and the legs quivering.

Augrabies Falls

5 November 1995

Maree: We cut loose this evening and dined in a restaurant, for the first time in months. We feasted on cordon bleu, Greek salad and a bottle of Craig Hall Chardonnay. The evening was calm and the sunset incredibly beautiful.

6 November 1995

Maree: This morning we had breakfast with squirrels and rock hyrax running around our feet. The baboons here are quite a problem, particularly one large male. They are quite adept at ambushing and bluffing the rather nervous tourists. A young guy camped near us is doing a field study of reptiles and in his spare time amuses himself by teasing the baboons. His trick is to put a rubber snake in a cornflakes box and then watch the impulsively curious baboons react. He places the box on the open grass and it is only a matter of minutes before the baboons get an uncontrollable urge to steal it. They open the end of the box to peer inside and on seeing the 'snake', drop it like a hot potato and run off screaming in the opposite direction. To them, real or not, it's a snake.

Kalahari-Gemsbok National Park

8 November 1995

Maree: After setting up camp, I cooked a pot of chow mein and as it was too hot to put in the freezer I left it in the pot under the car, with two heavy rocks on the lid to keep hungry animals away. The ploy nearly didn't come off, as a desert fox made determined efforts during the night to get at the food. I had to get up and rescue it as the cheeky fox sat watching me from a distance of about six metres. We did our best to continue our sleep with the strong smell of chow mein wafting through the car, as the only place it was safe was on the front seat. The bore water here was so mineralised it was undrinkable even with a heavy dash of sweet cordial. The flies would be best not mentioned.

9 November 1995
Brian: Tonight a brilliant moonrise, full and yellow, breaking above the flat horizon, through the few trees . . . and coming up so quickly you almost felt the earth turning.

10 November 1995
Brian: We see a lioness carrying a cub! Just a four-second sighting of her with the cub in her mouth before she disappeared from sight again into the bush. It was an extremely lucky and exciting sighting. Travelling along a corrugated, undulating road about three kilometres from Unie-End, Maree spotted three cheetah to the right of the car, resting in the shade. They were nervous of people and cars, as they crouched low on the ground with a 'worried' look in their eyes. They soon made a run for it across the dry white river bed of the Nossob and up over a sandy ridge into Botswana.

12 November 1995
Maree: Heading back towards Twee-Fontein, along a gravel road, I had an interesting race with an ostrich. Some animals, particularly ostriches and zebra, when they are on one side of your vehicle and wish to get to

the other, will race alongside trying to edge in front—so they can make a dash across the road. I have never seen one pull up and wait to cross after you pass. This particular ostrich and I raced for about 1.5 kilometres, and he was cruising. After a while he changed into top gear and surged ahead.

Upington, Northwest South Africa

13 November 1995

Brian: Most South Africans we have met across the country have gone out of their way to be friendly and helpful. It's been a good lesson for me in never judging people from afar through the media. I didn't have a good opinion of South Africans before I came here, but since living among them, I must say I learned to reserve my opinion in a big way.

Getting the Value Added Tax back on some goods we bought in South Africa (R1000 refund)—no way! We were sent to a travel agent in a restaurant, he sent us to the Magistrate's Office, they sent us to the Home Affairs Office where we stood in a queue for over an hour. We were sent from there to the Customs Office, who told us it was an Internal Revenue matter and that they don't have an office in Upington or the Namibian border. By then we had the message—they don't want to or can't refund tourists their VAT, which they say they will in the tourist brochures.

Fish River Canyon, Namibia

15 November 1995

Brian: It was an awe-inspiring sight to see the magnitude of the canyon and how the river had carved so deep a chasm (more than 1000 metres deep) and exposed the prehistoric layers of earth and rock, twisting every kilometre or so like a giant serpent (it's also seventy-five kilometres long!). It is surely one of the geological wonders of Africa, along with Victoria Falls and Kilimanjaro and the Nile (maybe also the Congo River, which we haven't seen).

Sesriem, Namib Desert

17 November 1995

Brian: The dunes appear from behind craggy rock hills and mountains, the colour of smoked salmon. We have never seen anything before like this unique landscape. It's impossible not to be impressed: the soft undulations of the massive surface of the dunes and the slightly burnt orange colour in the harsh glare of the afternoon sun—continuing in one unbroken profile for more than sixty kilometres and in direct contrast to the beautiful harsh outline of the Makuleft Mountains in the east.

18 November 1995

Brian: Heading for Walrus Bay on the Skeleton Coast while crossing the Namib Desert, a 'mirage' far away turned into a young white guy on a pushbike in the middle of the bloody desert! We couldn't believe it! He was pedalling with a very vigorous leg action, saddlebags and water bottles draped over the bike (all his worldly possessions?)—propelling himself along at an impressive ten kilometres per hour. And we thought that we were adventurous souls, hurtling along at 100 kilometres per hour, air conditioner on, in a Land Rover.

Windhoek

19 November 1995

Maree: Sometime during the night we were woken by the sound of some serious munching going on around the vehicle and looked out to find about twenty wildebeest grazing around us. They were so intent on feeding, their horns were gently 'clinking' on the car as they bumped into it.

20 November 1995
Maree: The bird life is very tame here and as we had breakfast we were joined by a pair of Egyptian geese and some guinea fowl which acted more like domestic chooks.

23 November 1995
Maree: We had a most unusual alarm call this morning—the sound of peacocks running around on the roof of our vehicle and peeking in at us through the small window above the door. Last night they had joined us for dinner. There were two males, one with his tail feathers cut off, a female and a motley group of youngsters.

Etosha National Park

24 November 1995
Maree: At the waterhole, we sat for a long time watching a big old male rhino and a younger one. As they stood facing one another at the water's edge they gave a perfect mirror image reflection in the pool. Even if my photos don't turn out, I will only have to shut my eyes to recall this beautiful sight. They took a long time to drink, as if they were savouring every drop.

25 November 1995
Maree: At the first waterhole we visited we witnessed two lions mating. We sat there for over an hour and they mated three times at intervals of about twenty minutes.

The male was a bit light in condition—but no wonder! I'm sure that food was the last thing on his mind. He had paid a price for 'his woman' as he had a lot of recent scars and wounds on his face, the result of fights with other males who were vying for her attention.

26 November 1995
Maree: Happy Birthday, Maree! It's my first African birthday—although I will miss having a drink with Anne [my best friend], who has always been with me in Sydney on this date. I'm sure she has found an excuse to open a bottle to celebrate for me.

After breakfast we drove to our third campsite in Etosha—Camp Namutoni—and enjoyed some more nice sightings at waterholes along the way. We watched a lone bull elephant having a delightful time at one, and when he moved off we drove around to intercept his retreat (I wanted a photo). He was quite relaxed until he stepped out of the bush onto the road in front of us. Then he suddenly swung around to face us, giving us the big 'piss off' signal—ears forward and trunk curled. Further on we saw large groups of zebra, gemsbok and wildebeest grazing on a vast open plain and as we approached another waterhole we saw thirty giraffe (one tiny baby) making their way across an open area. I have never before seen as many giraffe in one group.

Xahanaxa Camp, Okavango Delta

3 December 1995
Maree: The storm finally cleared and we headed out for another drive—seeing lots of giraffe, a few buffalo and a very large group of elephants with babies. On the way back to camp we again saw the elephants, making haste across the marsh heading towards the forest and led by

a young bull. They looked like they were late for an appointment as they scurried silently across our path. During the night we were again visited by the hyena as he clattered around the rubbish tip. He was the biggest hyena I have ever seen and hardly glanced at us as we tried to chase him away.

7 December 1995

Maree: We woke up at five-thirty this morning and got on the road to Savuti early, as we expected it to be extraordinary after yesterday's rain. It was—full of large pools of water and impossible (without wading in) to judge how deep the holes were. We crawled along at twenty-five kilometres per hour for the first hour, continually engaging diff. lock. Then the shit hit the fan—and we were bogged down in black cotton soil, all four wheels. Out came the shovel and Brian dug for nearly an hour while I packed leaves and branches in front and behind all four wheels. We unpacked all our gear to lighten the load before Brian got into the car—with fingers crossed. 'Bessie' gave a few grunts and moans but finally dragged herself out of the hole. All this time we were keeping a keen look-out for lions, but luckily saw none. We were relieved to eventually reach North Gate, the northern exit of the park. Here we were again held up as the bridge was down and the Parks Board guys were busy doing repairs. We were told the work would continue until at least the next day so we decided to stay in the campsite this side of the river. Ironically, the river is called the Kwai River, so we were amused to be stranded while the repairmen rebuilt 'the Bridge over the River Kwai'.

We have done a full circle in our African travels since first coming here in 1987. Kwai River was the first camp we ever stayed in, and after all we have seen, this area still ranks as one of the most beautiful in Africa. It is like a giant parkland with huge trees and spacious grasslands. As you look through the forest you feel as if you are inspecting a well-tended garden. The red leaves lie like a carpet on the ground and there are squirrels in abundance. There are so many impala with tiny babies, one to two days old. They stand staring at us with curious eyes and we realise we are probably the first humans they have seen. Brian notes the carcass of a large baboon high up in a tree.

4 December 1995
Brian: This morning we awaken to the lovely sight of many impala antelope and their tiny newborn young, grazing around the camp.

6 December 1995
Maree: We visited a borehole where we had sat eight years ago and been fascinated by the variety of wildlife. Now it is just a dry dugout as the elephants have destroyed the pump which used to fill it. Savuti is so different from the last time here. Back then, it was so dry, sandy, hot and the trees were all bare. Now, after so much rain, the trees have come alive and the ground is covered in a green carpet. But because of this, the animals are spread all over and difficult to see. A herd of zebra came galloping into camp, saw us, and quickly turned on their heels and headed back where they came from.

Brian: Tonight we sat down with a bottle of De Wet Wynkedler Sauvignon Blanc (South African) and watched a mighty display of Mother Nature, of lightning, thunder and swirling clouds to the west. As we sat and drank our wine (my glass was a recent casualty, so I had to drink from the thermos lid) a big hyena came loping past our position in the camp. I gave my 'cough' hyena whooping call as he passed, which seem to compound his confusion, so he kept running on, glancing back at short intervals, probably thinking, definitely not one of ours! After the rain had eased we stood around the fire, which surprisingly hadn't gone out . . . standing around a fire in the bush, gazing into it, seems to soothe the soul.

7 December 1995
Brian: The last time that we were here in 1987, the country was so dry that the animals were totally dependent on one water supply, a pump near the camp. The trees and bushes then were seemingly dead, stripped by the elephants to the point that the remaining branches and stems resembled grotesque arthritic fingers beseeching the heavens to send rain, while the 'whirly devils' whipped up dry hot sand and dust in grim testimony that this land was 'finished'! But what Nature appears to destroy is really only an adjustment in Her entire plan—in which time doesn't have the same meaning that humankind understands. Seeing this transformation of the Chobe National Park convinces us further that man shouldn't interfere with Nature—only to try to safeguard and expand what is left from the relentless and prolific destruction committed by humankind so far.

The Chobe National Park and Okavango Delta, from our observations travelling through Africa, have to be the wildest and most beautiful wildlife reserves in Africa and maybe the world.

Campsite Sinamatella, Hwange, Zimbabwe

11 December 1995

Maree: The evening was calm and we watched a thunderstorm on the horizon. The guy looking after the campsite came over to us for a chat, offering to collect firewood, do washing and ironing or any little job which would earn him a little extra. He has a wife and two kids but is also responsible for his sister-in-law and her eight kids as his brother died two years previously. It must be an awful struggle for some of these people as his wage would be considerably less than a park ranger's—but he seemed to handle it all with a sublime acceptance. 'It is life. What can I do?' he said. His manner was pleasant and courteous, with no sign of bitterness.

12 December 1995

Maree: We went for a drive this morning, again not seeing much, but we did find a few elephants, one of which was a bit *kali* [fierce], hiding behind a bush and looking for an excuse to have a go at us. When we didn't give him one (we had actually reversed) he came out onto the road, flapping his ears and shaking his head and spinning around as if daring us to take him on!

Back in camp it was the usual jobs for us: Brian cleaning the car and me with my bloody never-ending washing. Later, while relaxing, we produced a packet of nuts to munch on and found ourselves surrounded by squirrels. One, who had already eaten four or five, kept bolting off to a tree then returning to beg for more. We realised that he was stashing the nuts. The more I ignored him, the cheekier he got. He was actually running up my leg and sitting on this diary as I write, trying to get the nuts out of my hand. It's cute and amusing but at the same time it worries me to see animals a little too trusting in mankind.

14 December 1995
Maree: At a picnic spot Brian had a close encounter with a green mamba (one of Africa's deadliest). He was heading for the loo when he heard a hiss in the drain behind the toilet and looked across to see the snake. He called me, and some guys who were doing some maintenance work also came over. One of them threw a lump of dirt at it and the bloody thing headed straight for me. With a loud cry of 'shit', I high-stepped in the opposite direction—luckily for me, the snake did the same.

16 December 1995
Maree: We spent most of the day in the Motopos National Park, which is a small but beautiful park. This is the place, when he saw it for the first time, that Cecil Rhodes decided he would like to make his last resting place. He is buried on a high, rocky outcrop in the centre of the park. The rock formations are quite amazing here. It looks like some ancient giant has played with the huge rocks as if they were pebbles and stacked them one on top of the other. How they have stayed in place defies all logic.

18 December 1995
Maree: We arrive at the National Parks office for our appointment only to be told by the secretary that Mr Makombe is never in his office on Monday mornings. These people have an amazing ability to get you running around in bloody circles, chasing your tail. We head back to the Bronte Hotel with definite feelings of 'sod Africa' and the whole damned thing. I'm sure

some of these people could drive you stark raving mad in a couple of years—and the disconcerting thing is that they do it in such a pleasant manner.

19 December 1995
Maree: You read stories in the paper every day about councillors and mayors being taken to court for demanding bribes (or 'presents', as they call them) from people wanting to start a business or needing some kind of licence. It's endemic throughout Africa. We now feel that there is nothing we can do in this country to help the rhino and other endangered species. Our well-meaning attempts would be crushed by officialdom and our money used to line the pockets of politicians—not the stomachs of animals. My feeling now is one of 'God help Africa'.

Mutare
20 December 1995
Maree: While in town we were pestered by three white drunks outside the supermarket—one of whom tried to pull the old 'you ran over my foot' trick as we reversed out of the parking space. After getting no reaction (or money) other than cold stares from both of us, he walked, without limp, back to his mates. It was very unusual to see white derelicts in Africa.

Nyanga
22 December 1995
Brian: We spoke with a South African woman we met today about black rhino. She felt that they would all be gone by the turn of the century. The pessimism about the lack of government controls and resolve, and the ever-advancing tide of human population, is echoed throughout the continent, wherever we go.

Lake Kariba, Zimbabwe

23 December 1995

Maree: We finished dinner and sat down to watch the thunderstorms building up on three sides of us. It was cool, calm. Not a breath of air. Then, very suddenly, the breeze picked up . . . it was the wind of an approaching storm. We made a move to fold the awning away along with the chairs and table. But within the space of thirty seconds we were caught in the most furious wind I have ever experienced. We later realised this must have been the culmination of the winds off the three storms coming from different directions—and meeting right where we happened to be. The fire which had burned down to a solid bed of coals was violently blown out of the fireplace and we were caught in a hail of swirling, glowing coals as we battled in the wind to get the awning folded away into the bracket on the side of the 4 x 4. I stood back, horrified, as Brian struggled to get the jerrycans out of the way—and watched as he and the car were showered by the coals. For one horrible moment I thought the whole thing would explode.

24 December 1995

Maree: The storms raged all around us again in the evening and it was quite lovely to watch the sky lighting up as we sat having a Christmas Fosters, wondering what everyone at home was doing, as it was the dawn of Christmas Day in Australia.

25 December 1995

Maree: Christmas morning. We wake up to find the lid on the fridge ajar and that the battery, having worked overtime to keep it cool, had finally run down. This, of course, meant no cold drinks and soppy butter—and that all the stew and chow mein I cooked yesterday would not survive long. Merry bloody Christmas!

We couldn't be bothered going for a drive to recharge the freezer so we turned the ignition on and let it idle for one and a half hours. That did the trick and everything is now cold again. Christmas dinner consisted of stew and rice and our last bottle of South African wine.

27 December 1995
Maree: We left main camp this morning to drive to Sinamatella on the other side of Hwange. On the way we came across a lion kill. One very large male lion with an impressive salt and pepper mane and four females had brought down a giraffe right in the middle of the road. They had all fed and were resting, bellies full, in the shade just to the right of the kill. We pulled up next to a guy from South Africa and spent a couple of hours chatting to him as we watched the lions. Another car pulled up just behind us and the idiot driver decided to get out for a better look. The male lion suddenly changed from his sleepy, relaxed manner. His head came up, his eyes glowing as he positioned himself for a charge. He growled a bit before letting go with a thunderous roar and lunged forward two strides before stopping, striking the ground with his huge paws. He stopped short of a charge but it was an impressive display. The guy was back in his car in no time flat, and drove off, only to be shortly replaced by another car. This time, the parents sat in the front and allowed their child, about twelve, to climb out the back window and stand upright on the door frame. Once again the lion repeated the threat display. It's really hard to understand

the complacency of some of these people. The lion could have had the kid in two or three seconds—long before he could have got back into the car.

Victoria Falls

31 December 1995

Maree: We spent New Year's Eve at a huge party (3000 people!), taken there by our friends Leon and Mags Varley with whom we had been on walking safaris a few years earlier. It was held at the local school where they had three marquees and one of South Africa's top bands playing. The school puts the party on each year to raise money. Last year, with the proceeds, they were able to fence the entire school, to keep the lions and buffalo out. Leon and Brian stayed up all night—until seven o'clock in the morning—solving all the problems of Africa.

3 January 1996

Maree: A big day today—white-water rafting on the Zambezi. After a few quick lessons on safety we climbed onto our raft with our lifejackets and helmets on and set off for the day. The trip consisted of twenty-three rapids, which really got the adrenalin going. In between we floated calmly along the peaceful stretches of water. It was something I had always wanted to do on previous trips but never got around to. This section of white water is considered to be the best one-day rafting experience in the world. We managed to make the trip without getting thrown out—as many others did.

4 January 1996

Maree: Brian has lost a stone since starting the trip but hopefully all the steaks and veggies he is getting into at the moment will improve his condition.

Livingstone Camp in Zambia

6 January 1996

Brian: The guy who manages the camp worked in Australia for twelve years, at Byron Bay in New South Wales, and has been in Zambia for two years. I quizzed him for over an hour, and he painted a 'slow moving, tough going' picture of doing business in this country which doesn't surprise us, considering we have gained a much deeper and more enlightened insight into the working pulse of Africa during our nine months here.

24 January 1996

Brian: This morning we leave Pete Giraudo's house (at Langata, near Nairobi), en route to Uganda and stay the night in an 'African' hotel (blacks only) at Eldoret in western Kenya. Everything in the hotel is old but very clean and at 700 KSH (AUS$18) per night is quite suitable, as accommodation is hard to find. We observe that it has a 'facility' for ladies of the night, which is amusing. How our hotel standards have dropped in the last twelve months or so! Pete Giraudo is an old and dear friend who we first met on safari in Kenya in the 1980s with Marcus Russell. Pete is a well-read and educated bloke and I used to love talking to him about Africa—the politics, wildlife, people, religions and future directions. Whenever we were in Nairobi, he afforded us the same sort of generous hospitality that Jamie Roberts did.

Uganda

30 January 1996

Maree: At a service station just before the border we were approached by an old beggar who rambled on in Swahili about how hungry he was and that he had no money for food or tea. As he spoke to me I was doing my best to pretend I couldn't understand as I was enjoying his impressive performance; I could actually understand everything he was saying. It was all I could do to keep a straight face. Brian gave him a couple of dollars and was rewarded with a huge grin and salute. 'I salute you, sire,' he said, in English.

At Lake Barringo tonight we had a lovely dinner with Betty Roberts, Jamie's mum, and afterwards, as we sat on the verandah, a hippo wandered up from the lake to feed on the lawn in front of us.

Naivasha

1 February 1996

Maree: We saw a leopard on a bait which had been placed in a tree two kilometres from the camp. We watched as the silhouette of the leopard slithered down the trunk of the tree, then we scooted back to camp to retrieve the flashlight. When we returned we caught sight of the leopard under some bushes and, as we drove in for a closer look, we got stuck on loose sand. There was nothing to do but get out of the car and dig our way out—while keeping the spotlight firmly on the leopard as it watched us from under the bush. The hyenas made a hell of a racket all night as they hunted near camp.

2 February 1996

Maree: You wouldn't believe what we did this morning: we actually went to watch trackwork!! A couple we met last night, Jilly and Tom Fraser, have about fourteen horses in work. We went to their house, which was just up the road, for a drink before dinner. Tom made a friend for life out of me by producing some Fosters, and Jilly picked Brian's brains about horseracing in Australia.

They invited us to come see the horses work this morning. The track was basically a dirt circumference with a long straight, set out on the shores of Lake Naivasha, and we had to do a lap of the track in the Land Rover first to chase away the giraffe. That was definitely a first for us. Jilly and Tom are both very enthusiastic about their horses and racing, despite very poor facilities and lousy prize money.

Ivan Tomlinson's property, seventy-five kilometres northwest of Nanyuki

10 February 1996

Brian: We have 90 per cent made up our minds that we will try another twelve months here. Yesterday we went to Lewa Downs, which is now a famous rhino sanctuary in Kenya, to meet Fuzz Dwyer, the manager there. We had had a meeting with him before we went on our safari down south and he asked us to come and see him when we returned. While waiting for him to finish working with a film crew, we went for a drive around Lewa, and saw lots of animals (elephants, rhino and most of the usual African game), the most interesting of all being a male and female cheetah which are being reintroduced into the wild after being in a zoo in Mombasa. Fuzz discussed a business venture—running a tourist camp in a new wildlife area which adjoins Lewa Downs to the north. We are going to investigate the details of that.

25 February 1996

Brian: We have been in the camp at Ivan's for three nights now and have found inactivity a problem, giving us too much time to think. The result has been that we have decided we can't see too much future in this and have started talking about going home for good . . . although I feel that after being home five or six weeks we are going to be in the same situation, mentally, as when we left. I don't want to go into the same old routine and faces of racing.

The campsite itself is a very beautiful place, with its massive rocks and palm trees, and the sound of the hidden waterfall as a backdrop. It's especially beautiful in the early morning and late evening. We worry and wonder if there would be enough animals to keep tourists interested if we went to all the expense of setting up a good camp here. There are plenty of animals at different times, but they don't appear at all times in plentiful numbers, which is what the tourists like, the fact being that they are usually only in the camp for a few days.

26 February 1996
Brian: We have an African guy, a Samburu, living in a tent nearby, who acts as a helper and watchman for us while we are away. He got a bit panicky towards sundown, when a group of elephants moved close to his campsite near the river. He was yelling at them to let them know that there were people nearby. This only seemed to infuriate a young bull, who started to adopt a charge posture, so I let out a few resounding Aussie 'cooees' which seemed to effectively confuse the elephant as he shook his big head and ears, with what appeared from a distance to be a puzzled look in his eye. He then turned and moved back into the bush with purposeful footsteps!

28 February 1996
Brian: On a game drive this morning after being woken by the Egyptian geese 'alarm clock', this is what we saw:

four giraffe, one warthog, two bat-eared foxes, three augar buzzards chasing a goshawk in flight, a few groups of impala, three klipspringers (small rock antelope) and quite a few dik dik antelope near the camp.

5 March 1996
Brian: The moonrise was very beautiful, at 7.00 p.m. from behind a large mass of clouds in the east. The night was quite noisy with the calling of the lions from 7.30 p.m. right through until six o'clock the next morning. There seemed to be about six of them; three just across the river, two about 180 metres downriver and one behind us about 360 metres away. So our tent was virtually 'surrounded' for the night. Their noise woke us a few times. We also heard hyena and hippos.

6 March 1996
Brian: At dinner time we had some curried sausages (beautiful!) and while we were eating we saw two klip-springers way up high on a massive rock, looking down at us. Another magic moment.

11 March 1996
Brian: The 'can't stops' (the runs) struck me at 11.30 p.m. and there was a dash for the 'thunderbox' followed by the thought, 'to hell with the lions'. I hoped that they had eaten earlier! The strange white object that appeared about ground level may have confused them in the half-moonlight (I didn't make it to the thunderbox!). It was an interesting observation on civilised man—he would rather risk being eaten by an animal than acting like one. It's probably the basic reason why so many 'civilisations' eventually decline.

My problem was responsible for me seeing the first

light of the African dawn. Another call came early and again I was out, on my stiff-legged, steady-as-you-go gait (almost made it!). After everything had been 'sorted out', I saw the spectacle of the eastern sky bathed in brilliant gold with stripes of dark cloud across it. Away to the north stood a large mass of clouds like a thunderhead, which glowed soft pink on a massive backdrop of slate-grey cloud. The birds provided the background music and, in spite of the absence of a conductor, sounded wonderful. The air was fresh and still.

Chapter Twenty

Out of Africa

We came back from Africa in 1996 disillusioned and disappointed—and feeling a great sense of loss. Over there, we knew, was a life that we really wanted and enjoyed. But we hadn't been able to hold onto it . . . it had slipped through our fingers.

Not long after I came back to Australia for good—after a brief return trip to Nairobi to sell the Land Rover and the camping equipment, we called in to see some old friends, Pat Webster (the Randwick trainer) and his wife Chrissy. 'What are you going to do?' Pat asked me.

'I really don't know,' I answered. 'We might try and do something with wildlife.'

Even on the last, short, sad trip to Africa I was still looking around for something that might suit us. Hoping. Maree and I had left everything in storage to come back to Sydney to get a 'gut feeling' about things. We reflected, weighed everything up, and ultimately decided it was not financially viable to stay in Africa. So I flew back, sold our things—something of a nightmare exercise in a place like Nairobi, and taking six weeks in all, such were the difficulties. I don't want people to think we gave up. We gave it our best shot. We put our lives on the line . . .

At that time there was no thought of going back to the racing world, which I believed I had left forever. It turned out that Pat and Chrissy Webster had recently bought a property, Belinfante, out between Gulgong and Mudgee in western New South Wales, and not so far from Dubbo, where we had a strong association with the Western Plains Zoo. 'Why don't you go up there,' they said. 'Stay as long as you like.'

It was the pause we needed, a chance to step away and think. Over the preceding months we had become pretty good at that. Africa embraces you in that way, and as Maree said—and she's right—the experience brought calmness and a different attitude to my life. Sitting around an African campfire at night, there is a lot of time for thinking, for soul-searching.

The attitude of the African people had changed me too. I became much better at letting things flow, letting them happen when they were ready to happen, rather than making a big deal of things. People over there never do anything in a hurry, because if they do it in a hurry, it is done with—and they sit twiddling their thumbs. Even their greetings can go on forever. Their attitude is 'that can wait' or 'we'll do it in our time'. Initially, it used to anger me, but then I just relaxed and accepted that that was the way it was, and went along with them. That was one of the biggest benefits I got out of Africa, to be able to accept just 'going with the flow'. Time is nothing over there. There is daylight, and there is dark, and life just rolls along.

So we went to the Websters' country retreat, and stayed

five months. Over the days we painted the big old rambling homestead inside and did up the gardens. And we thought about the future. We travelled around, looking at different places that were set up as wildlife areas for native Australian animals, checking out properties, getting prices. I reached the conclusion that going into property was a very expensive way of buying a lifestyle, and that setting up some sort of wildlife sanctuary was not really the way to go because even if it happens to be successful, somewhere down the track—when you die or decide you can't go on any more—you have all these captive animals that someone has to do something with. People at the Dubbo zoo talked to us about that problem. Our conclusion was that we would have been creating a potential problem which would be directly contrary to our objectives with wildlife.

With some reluctance, as 1996 unfolded, I arrived gradually at the decision that I would go back into racing, the sport/business I knew best. I said to Maree: 'It will be hard starting from scratch again, but maybe we can look at it from the point of view that it is just another way of helping wildlife by raising money. We'll try it, and see how well we do.' I reached the conclusion that I needed to stick to something I knew, and that I needed a goal. I was fifty years of age.

At that point I began to look closely at how things were in Australian racing, and decided that Victoria was doing much better, overall, than the other states in areas such as management and prize money. I figured that if I was going to start a business from scratch, I'd be better off starting in an area that was buoyant. I was unimpressed with the New South Wales Government's attitude to racing at that time, believing it to be all take-out, with little put-back. 'They just continue to milk it dry,' I told a journalist. 'They are letting New South Wales racing wither on the vine.'

Around Christmas time 1996, we went and stayed with

Maree's parents at Warrnambool and from there I began the process of 'networking', between Warrnambool and Melbourne, to re-establish myself as a trainer. I got lucky—as I had now and then in the past—but this time it was more to do with my name and reputation than with fate's hand. There weren't any stables available when I first wanted them, but I probably received priority treatment over a couple of others, and eventually got the nod for six new stables being built at Flemington, nice big boxes, well insulated and with plenty of light.

I had six boxes to start with, then after a few months another nine became available. Eighteen months later I had another nine built, taking me up to twenty-four. And that's what it is today. My new base was on the flat alongside the Melbourne Cup start near the top of the straight six. Subsequently, when Clarrie Connors decided to shift to Caulfield, I was offered his boxes, adjoining mine, which would have taken my numbers up to forty. I thought about it, and said 'no'.

I had been on the treadmill of being a big trainer, and I just didn't want to do that again. With twenty-four horses in work, I knew I was not going to make a great impression on racing. But it was what I decided to do. Even with that scaled-down approach, I felt a sense of 'going back over old ground'.

When I returned to racing, I didn't have a thing, not even a bridle, as I'd sold all my gear in 1995, so it was a case of starting absolutely from scratch. My return to training, and the restart in Melbourne rather than Sydney, generated some publicity—and some old friends came out of the woodwork to give me horses. Jack Eastgate gave me Wry Hero, a testy sprinter which hadn't won a race for eighteen months, and a fellow named Des Pope came around with Great Condor, which was a bit of a cripple and hadn't won for more than a year. Rob Ferguson and Peter Joseph from Sydney sent horses to me, and so did the likes of Geoff Wild and Evan Spurling and my old mentors, Robert Sangster and Bob Lapointe.

It was an entirely fresh start. My record read that I had trained around 2000 career winners, including twenty-two Group 1 winners and 132 victories in stakes races. But none of that mattered as I 'started again' . . .

As it turned out, my return was fairytale stuff, better by far than I could have hoped for. Wry Hero (7/1) was my first runner back (on 12 July 1997), and he blitzed a big field down the straight at Flemington to win the 1200 metres Collex Waste Handicap by three and a half lengths, keeping intact my record of having won with my first runner at tracks all the way down the coast: Cairns, Townsville, Sydney, and now Melbourne.

It was a carefully planned exercise. I had walked the track on the Thursday and Friday before the race, keeping a close eye on the weather to make sure all was 'right' for Wry Hero, a bad-tempered gelding, whose disposition progressively improved with the TLC we gave him.

Things got even better, with Great Condor winning twice in succession in Straight Six races at Flemington as my second and third starter back as a trainer, the second win coming in a Group 3 race worth $100,000. So the record (in town) stood at three runners, three winners. If I was going to come back to racing, I guess this was the way to do it.

Funny thing was, in double-quick time it felt like I had never been away. I was straight back into the routine, because I had to be. And the routine of life is, of course, the trap. It sucks you back in—the TV, the newspapers—and suddenly you're back where you were. Sometimes, as I worked in the stable, it was as if the African adventure had never happened. But to (re-)start the way I did in Melbourne gave me a good sense of achievement and satisfaction. To emerge from the depths of Africa and go 'bang'—that felt pretty good. Melbourne, after all, was a new horizon for me, and new horizons have always been very important in my life.

Let's face it, I've been a wanderer ever since I was born—to the point where it's hard for me to identify with anywhere as 'home'. Ask me where I regard as home, and I'll tell you that I don't know any more. I suppose you always think first of the place where you grew up. But that was so long ago . . . and if I went back to Cairns now, it would have changed so much that I doubt it would feel much like home to me any more.

By 2000, my stable had built up to between sixty-five and sixty-eight horses 'on the books' at any time, with twenty-four in work at Flemington. When my secretary, Melissa, tallied up the winners in mid-year 2000, it came to 102 since my return to racing, for a strike rate of 4.8. In that were fifteen stakes, group and black-type races, with horses like Oliver Twist, Sedation, Special Dane and Wry Hero. As a three year old, Special Dane won a Group 1 race for me, the CF Orr Stakes in 1998, beating an out-and-out champion in Might and Power. A classy Danehill colt, he also won the $150,000 Sandown Guineas in 1997.

The press described me as 'nearly overcome with emotion' when Oliver Twist, as 4/1 favourite, won the Group 111, $100,000 Coongy Handicap (2000 metres) at Caulfield in late December 1999. It was true enough. Jim Cassidy rode the horse for me and our success turned the clock back to our halcyon days in Sydney. Inevitably, I remembered that time, and talked of the 'past revisited': 'I've always said Jim was the best jockey ever to ride for me and I stand by that,' I told pressmen. 'We've had our disagreements, the odd blue, but I've always respected him. It feels great . . . it feels right to have Jim riding for me again.' I rated Cassidy's ride that day as 'ten out of ten'.

Along the way of my 'comeback' there have been moments, such as that one, that I have enjoyed immensely, yet I'd be lying if I said I was over the moon about being back doing what I'm doing. I seem to be going all the time—I feel imprisoned again to an extent. And I miss Africa. To be tied down after having had the freedom of those couple of years (1995–96) is bloody hard. And when you're not broke—and we're fairly comfortable—and don't *have* to do it, it's even harder to accept. And the thing is that, unless I fluke a couple of really good horses, it never is going to get much better than it has been. I apply myself, work darned hard and do the very best I can with the horses I have—yet I have a feeling that there is no real direction in what I am doing. Sure, there is always the Melbourne Cup, a race I would dearly love to win—but the odds on that are long for a trainer with twenty-four horses.

Winning the Cup is a dream I have held onto for many years. A dozen years ago I told a journalist in an interview: 'It's been a goal that's been way up there with me. If you went through your whole career and you looked back knowing that the Melbourne Cup wasn't among your wins—it would give your whole career an empty feeling.' I haven't given up on that, but my priorities have certainly changed.

The thing that drives me now is just this: the goal of raising money for wildlife. I know that the more successful I am as a trainer, the more help I will be able to provide. And that is a strong incentive. What I do in that area is nothing spectacular, but at least it gives me the satisfaction of knowing I am doing *some* good. And that is something that can drive a life. The main support that Maree and I provide is through the black rhino program at Western Plains Zoo. I believe that if you spread the money around too much—to too many organisations—it is spread too thin and you haven't got enough input into any one of them. We've been with the black rhino program virtually from its inception. Considering the difficulties, the zoo has done a fantastic job. They have got three live calves—although, sadly, they lost one when we were up at Dubbo at Easter, 2000. When you consider that these people have had to learn basically from scratch about breeding black rhino in captivity—and they're a notoriously difficult animal to breed from—they have done a wonderful job. We have been very happy to be associated with it in our small way.

So that's where it stands at the moment. The bloke who started training horses on a bush track up north almost thirty years ago is back training them again, caring as much for the animals in my stable now as I did back then. But the journey of the years has changed me. Reflecting on the return from Africa to racing, I said to Maree recently that I felt like someone who has left a familiar room and is now back in it, experiencing the same things he did before, notwithstanding the profound impact that Africa has had on me, and especially so in the trek of 1995–96.

So much is the same in my life. I have the same reaction to disappointment, I still relate to people in the rather awkward manner of previous years, I have the same frustrations. I take pretty much the same view of people and how I do my job that I took before. When one of my horses gets beaten or someone reacts to me in a certain way, I react the way I did before. Calmer, yes—because of the experience of Africa—but not so different really . . .

The disappointing thing about the whole scenario is that I haven't been able to *extend* that room I left. I have gone from it, done a bit of a buzz around, and come back to the confined space again. I feel as I did years ago. Yet I know that I *have* made my life a bit more colourful, doing the things that I have done, but the nagging thought is always there that I haven't expanded it that much, haven't added too much in the way of depth.

I think it's probably just life, the way it is, has been and will be—and I'm happy to say at least that the restlessness is still within me. It is that restlessness that has *made* things happen for me in my life. I think that when any of us reach the point where we say 'well, that's my lot', then we're surely not going to progress any further past that point. I'm not there yet, I'm happy to say.

I suspect at the end of the day that although there are frills and bells and whistles on the edges of some lives, everyone's life follows a roughly similar track. You read tales of adventurous lives, but I imagine those are *condensed* stories—featuring the highlights, plastered together—and, as it is for all of us, large slabs of those lives have been boring and mundane too. The twist in the tail is that it's the mundane and the routine that makes you appreciate the pleasures and the special moments.

And even when you do something like Maree and I did—tearing up something familiar and comfortable that we had, to have a shot at something edgy and different—then most often you still have to return, at some time, to the basic things. Even the blokes who climb Everest have to come back to earth and get jobs in the real world, before taking on the next challenge.

I am fortunate that I work with animals I love—horses—with the purpose of supporting the wildlife that I care so very much about. And I work outdoors; a beautiful sunrise glimpsed at the start of a working day at Flemington can still be something very special in a life. On my way back from the track, I see people getting into their cars, going to work—people sitting in their cars at the lights, crawling through the peak-hour traffic to the office . . . knowing they've got to do it all over again in reverse in the afternoon. That would drive me stir-crazy. I know I would just have to break out.

Compared with a lot of people, I know that Maree and I have had fortunate and fantastic lives. I wonder sometimes whether my restlessness is to do with maybe having had *too* much—of having built an expectation that things will just get better and better. And I wonder sometimes, too, whether I should just bloody settle down, accept what I've got and get on with life.

But, with the history of my fifty-three years so far, I know for sure it won't happen. I know deep down there is much still to be done. In fact, there is already another trip in my mind . . . before long. There always is. Never a day goes by that, at some time, I don't think of Africa.